ESCAPING COMMUNIST HUNGARY

Escaping Communist Hungary 1956

Irene Korponay

Published by Ryan von Schwedler

Escaping Communist Hungary 1956

Copyright © 2016 Ryan von Schwedler

All rights reserved under International and Pan-American Copyright Conventions

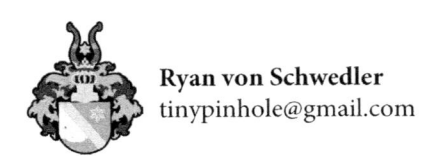

Ryan von Schwedler
tinypinhole@gmail.com

ISBN: 1512396001
ISBN-13: 978-1512396003

Printed in the United States of America by Createspace

I am dedicating my book to my daughter Rita, who was the heroin of the escape. She was seven years old and did not shed one tear during the difficulties of the escape from Hungary to the West. She endured sleeping on the floor of strange houses, walking miles in December over icy snowfields to freedom. Her face always remained calm throughout the ordeal.

I'm also dedicating this book to the wonderful American university students who waited endless hours on the Austrian border for the usual small groups of refugees arriving on the other side of the river. They pulled many boats to freedom. I'm sorry that I never learned their names.

CONTENTS

1. Kinga — 1
2. The Sterns — 15
3. Occupation Russian Style — 23
4. The Story of Ester — 41
5. Life After the Invasion — 55
6. Tibor — 67
7. Revolution — 75
8. Shattered Dreams — 89
9. Eva — 109
10. Ibi — 117
11. Rays of Hope — 121
12. The Escape — 125
13. The Second Escape — 137
14. Life in the Barracks — 163
15. The American Reporter — 181
16. Maca — 189
17. Epilogue — 215
18. Afterword — 219

Chapter One
KINGA

I WAS BORN AND RAISED in historical Esztergom, Hungary, which lies along the banks of the Danube. It has a tributary of the Danube flowing through its center with indigo-blue mountains on its horizon, medieval churches and the gigantic Basilica Cathedral on its highest hill, rows and rows of yellow, white, pink, and blue, pastel-colored baroque and rococo and renaissance houses on its steep streets under century-old chestnut, oak, and elm trees. The city is as precious to me as the pearls on the crown of our first King, Saint Stephen.

I am an only child and am named after a princess of the house of Arpad, the royal family for the first 300 years of Hungarian history! The princess lived in the thirteenth century and had the same high-cheekboned, wide-apart-eyed face as I have, and the same name, Kinga. Among the rows of leather-bound books in our well-stocked library of both European and foreign masterpieces, one contains an etching of the princess; she seems to have dreamy eyes, the only thing I find flattering as far as our resemblance goes.

My father operates the oldest winery in the city. He is rather a solitary man who lives only for us. My mother is a beautiful woman with violet eyes and thick reddish-blonde hair. An all conquering but sweet smile lights her soft face and disguises an extremely strong character. She is a surgeon in the local hospital, which stands surrounded by tall trees on a hill at the outskirts of the city. There she spends most of her time.

I am a happy child. I love Mother and Father. They love me as much as I love them, maybe even more.

We live in a long, greyish-white house, close to the Danube, across from the Palace of the Archbishop. In the manicured garden of the palace, priests and canons walk back and forth at all hours of the day, reading their breviaries.

The large rooms of our house have cathedral ceilings and whitewashed walls. They are filled with mahogany furniture shiny from years and years of polishing, hung with beautiful oil paintings, and scattered with silk and velvet pillows on the divans and on the floor. A baby-grand piano stands in the corner room, which opens onto a balcony of geraniums, and father and I play classical, folk and popular music there, and also receive guests. I love the relaxed, colorful, lively atmosphere of our house. I also love Grandma's house situated at the other end of the city, and there I spend a lot of time with my cousins. Grandma is my father's mother, a great old lady whom I adore. It is like a holiday to go to her big old stone house on Calvary Hill. It has many open verandas and glassed in ones, long rows of rooms, and a hanging garden filled with flowers and vegetables of every kind. Grandma is always busy at the other end of the house, where the big oval room is, and some of the verandas are reserved for her paying guests. She is both the chef and the manager of the restaurant, and became the breadwinner after Grandpa's death.

My favorite place is the wine cellar, which is cut deep into the foundation of the house. There I play hide and seek with my numerous cousins among the huge, sweet-smelling barrels of wine. I also love her immense kitchen with its amber-colored copper plates and pots hanging on the walls. Fires are always burning in the two big iron stoves. Lina, the old maid, and Ilona, the young one, prepare delicious dishes for us and for the paying guests. They are perpetually cooking and baking; their strong peasant faces shiny red from their perspiration and industry.

The smell of good food is an invitation to passersby; it lures in the customers, and it lingers throughout the house like a thick cloud. On weekends throngs of tourists arrive from Budapest on the steamboats. They come year after year after year, the same people filling the porches and the oval room with laughter and appeasing their insatiable appetites. When the tourists are very numerous, the entire family helps to serve them, including Mother and Father, carrying huge trays of food and beer and wine. And waitresses and waiters swarm all over the house and in and out of the kitchen.

Father is Grandma's favorite son. It gives her a lot of heartache that he is not well right now. He contracted tuberculosis on a business trip about a year ago. During a big winter storm he was trapped in his car in a village, where he had been looking for good wine to buy from the peasants. Since then his condition has deteriorated. He has a persistent cough and a constant low-grade fever. This worries Mother and Grandma, and also worries me.

Old Doctor Emanuel has warned Mother that Father will soon die. How long he is to be with us only God knows. Mother and I are trying to make the best of the situation in the meantime, trying to be with him as much as possible, talking and reading and playing the piano together and teasing our German Shepherd, Pityu, who loves us all with a deep passion.

Father is very interested in the history of our town. He has told me there is evidence that man lived here as early as prehistoric times, although the first known tribes were the Celts, who appeared in this area in the fourth century B.C. He said that I'd soon be learning about our history in school, but that he would love to tell me about it in more detail, if I was really interested. I begged him to teach me everything he knew.

Father told me that the Romans conquered the region in the first century A.D., making the city, which they named Solva, into a cornerstone of their defense. In the fifth century the Huns moved in, followed by the Avars and Moravians. Finally, in 986 A.D., the Hungarian tribes arrived led by Arpad. It was here that his grandson Vajk was born. He took the name Stephen when he became a Christian and he was crowned the first Hungarian king in 1001 A.D.

The history of our town fascinates me, as does the beautiful crown of King Saint Stephen, which is on display in the castle up on the hills of Buda. The crown is studded with diamonds and precious stones and glitters like a comet does in the August sky. In our library there are books about King Stephen, who made our city the capital of the new kingdom, which it remained for almost three centuries.

Father has read aloud to me stories about olden times, when there were beautiful castles in Hungary with elaborate gardens, when noblemen and their ladies dressed in velvet and silk walked in the moonlight, listening to the songs of the troubadours.

When the weather is good, we take walks in the city, usually choosing the streets, which still have the atmosphere of the past, dating back to Marcus Aurelius. We walk close to the Cathedral where archeologists have uncovered the ruins of thermal baths and beautiful villas, digging up dishes, vases, and water jugs, and jewelry made of copper and bronze.

I love both of my parents. But I adore my father because he is always at home. His illness prevents him from working.

Father often takes me to our favorite place, an archeological dig on the outskirts of the city. There is the headstone of a young girl, who, according to the inscription, was the daughter of a noble Roman named Jucundus. There she lies dreaming of long-past centuries in her grave underneath a willow tree.

Father and I talk incessantly about the past of our city and about everything else. He tells me that he will not be with us for long. Yet he believes that even after he is gone, he and I will remain together in spirit, and I find great comfort in this thought. I am terrified of losing him. He wants me to enjoy life, which I do to please him. And I am happy in the abundant love and attention I receive from him and from my Mother. I am sad and I am yet not sad; life tastes like drops of honey, because I am too young to dwell on suffering.

One day in the spring of 1943, my parents and I went to another favorite place, a small island clasped on all sides by "the Blue Danube." This small and lovely island was nameless; everyone just referred to it as "The Island." People loved to go there from the city on Sundays because of its lovely meadows and roads, filled with shrubs and trees and flowers of every kind. Everyone also loved the old, romantic-looking restaurant. The day we were there the landscape looked like the Watteau paintings in the museum. The meadows were starred with yellow dandelions and the young grass was the color of emeralds.

After sunset we went to the old restaurant, which beckoned us with its faded brown shutters and peeling walls. There we found many of our friends sitting round the long wooden tables in the stone-enclosed yard. They were eating cold fried chicken and homemade bread, which they had brought from home, and drinking beer and wine. We sat at the same table as the local pharmacist, Mr. Feher, and his wife Ilus who both taught music and piano in the high school. Mr. Piros and his family were also there with their aunts and uncles and their children. Everyone was happy and noisy, including Father who was in an especially good mood. We watched the sunset with its red and purple clouds, sang Hungarian folk songs, and generally enjoyed life. Father talked to me of his plans for the coming summer: we would all go hiking in the Pilis mountains, which were full of wild life and where the huge rocks stood deep-set in feather grass. "There, yellow irises in the swamp gaze at their reflections in the silver waters," he said. "It is a good place to take pictures of the wild ducks that float on the surface of the lake as though hypnotized." He would take pictures of Mother and me by the lake, he said, and he looked round the table and invited everyone to join us in the excursion.

Everyone was planning something for the summer. They seemed to be in love with life and with their beautiful city and its surroundings.

"All this beauty is a special gift of God," said Mother.

"We must take care, we must take good care of our city," said Mrs. Feher. We all drank to that, even the children, from small glasses of red wine, which tasted like nectar.

We laughed and laughed and Mr. Piros told jokes. But then Father began to cough so violently that mother handed him her fine white handkerchief. I was horrified when I saw the blood staining the white batiste to scarlet red. Mother sprang to her feet and announced that we must take Father to the hospital. Everyone looked alarmed and I burst into tears. So we took him to the hospital, where he was to stay for an entire year, returning, as we hoped, cured. Our life as a family became perfect again. Little did we know how short-lived our happiness would be. And no one guessed what sadness and destruction and tears the coming years would bring.

* * *

One month after Father came back from the hospital, we were sitting around in the kitchen while Mother brewed the coffee and Father and I watched her, waiting for breakfast. We were expecting Ilona, Grandma's maid, who always brought us fresh rolls from the bakery on her way to Grandma's. That particular morning she was very late and when she arrived, she looked frightened. Her face was very pale and she stood staring down at her bare feet on the cool brick floor of our kitchen as though bereft of words.

"What is the matter, Ilona? Is something the matter with Grandma?" cried Mother. But there was no reply.

At last she stammered, "The Germans. They are all over town, mostly on Main Street."

Father's face expressed disbelief, and "I don't understand," said Mother.

"I don't— I don't know," she said. "They are all over on Main Street, German soldiers and all. People are there, hundreds and hundreds of people, a large crowd gathered there on the sidewalks, watching."

Within a few minutes we, too, headed for Main Street, and sure enough we found a crowd of Hungarians standing on the sidewalks, staring in silence at the German Army just as Ilona had described.

"Ilona is right. This is the German Army," Mother muttered to herself. I, too, stared at the Germans who were growing in number in the middle of the street. Watching then as they sat stiffly on their army trucks holding their rifles, I wondered why everyone looked so worried. To me it was interesting and exciting. I could have stayed there forever watching the Germans.

Later in the day we heard on the radio that the Germans had occupied all the airports in Hungary, but no one really knew the whole story. For the next couple of days the city buzzed like a beehive with people discussing the situation in disbelief.

Father and I continued our daily walks, but it was no longer so pleasant, since the German soldiers seemed to occupy all the streets and squares, as well as the military barrack on Main Street.

"I have the terrible feeling that our life will be drastically changed," said Father. "The Germans will force us more and more into the war."

Instead of reading books and playing the piano, we now listened constantly to the radio while the events of the last few days slowly unfolded. People from the neighborhood and some of our relatives came day after day after day to our house to discuss the German invasion. As far as I was concerned, they made far too much fuss about the situation. They behaved as if the world had come to an end, while my cousins and I rather enjoyed all the excitement the Germans had brought with them. We sneaked out into the streets and spoke to the soldiers who stood guard in front of the military barrack, trying to show off our proficiency in the German language. At first Father scolded us, but then decided to explain things he thought it would be to our advantage to know. We learned that Hitler was dissatisfied with the halfhearted efforts of our Head of State, Admiral Horthy, and his government, and had decided to send troops into Hungary to put pressure on a reluctant ally. As a result, uncertainty swept through the country. Kallay, our premier, who had been secretly negotiating with the Western allies, had taken refuge in the Turkish Embassy in Hungary (Later he was to be smuggled out of Budapest and died in exile in New York). A new government had been formed under Stojay, previously Hungary's ambassador to Berlin, whom the Germans trusted. The situation was further complicated by the fact that the Soviet Army was already fighting German and Hungarian troops in Transylvania, the eastern part of Hungary.

After the German invasion several classes were canceled in the convent school, which I attended, and soon German soldiers were billeted in every house in the city that had a spare room. Three men were assigned to us whose names were Eric, Walter, and Sigmund, all of them blonde and square-faced. I rarely saw them as they kept to themselves in their room, listening to Radio Berlin, and sometimes playing sentimental tunes like "Billy Marlene" on their harmonicas. After a month they left to go to the Front. Others followed, young German soldiers who gave off a mixed aura of sentimentality, melancholy, and aggressiveness. In the meantime, my parents and I continued our everyday life as best we could.

Mother was busy at the hospital. Because school was still closed, I sat with father on the balcony with the geraniums, reading and listening to "Rigoletto" or "Aida" or "Lohengrin" (our favorites) on the Victrola; or we just sat in silence, enjoying each other's company.

It was on a rainy day that we first heard the sirens announcing an air raid. We ran to the basement of the nearby Saint Ladislaus Church, which had been assigned as a shelter to those who lived in the area. For hours we sat in darkness listening to the hissing of bombs. From that day on, we had air raids every day and were ordered to keep our windows blacked out with dark paper. American and British warplanes flew nightly above our heads in the star-studded sky and the city lay in darkness under a blanket of fear.

Eventually, Father made our own shelter in the cellar of our house. We carried down our mattresses and blankets, a kerosene burner, and some loose tea among other things. Here we spent many nights, watching the big water bugs that crawled unperturbed across the dirt floor, and listening to the screaming of the bombs.

The damp air aggravated Father's condition. He began to cough again, and he developed a fever, which he described as giving him a mild feeling of euphoria. This, Mother considered to be a bad sign. On account of the air raids, school was now closed down for good. I missed the pleasant atmosphere of the convent school, the incense-smelling lobbies and chapels, the new wing with its bright classrooms, and, above all, the rose garden in the courtyard surrounded by its high stone walls, where I could chat endlessly with the other girls.

The city was pretty quiet, but we didn't have a dull moment in politics. On October 15th the Nazis took over, and the next day I had an invitation to Aunt Katinka's birthday, to be held at Grandma's house. Anticipating a fine afternoon with Russian tea, *Dobos Torte*† and glazed macaroons, I left home early and took a short cut through Szecheny Square.

The Square looked unusually empty when I got there. There was something sinister in the stillness of the surroundings, the quietness of the stone houses. Not a soul was in sight, not even at the windows, where people usually stood watching the passersby for entertainment. There was absolutely no one around, with the exception of a half-dozen horse-drawn wagons standing by the beautiful twelfth century mansion of Blind General Bottyan, a nobleman and a famous military leader of the Rakoczi uprising against the Hapsburgs in 1705.

Just then a few uniformed men came out of one house and stood under the elm trees as if waiting. I hid behind the statue of the Holy Trinity in order to check out the situation. I didn't have to wait long. People started to emerge from the houses, walking slowly as if paralyzed and escorted by uniformed Nazis. They walked toward the wagons, the soldiers pushing them and shouting harsh orders. I recognized Mr. and Mrs. Schreiber among them, and their

---

† Hungarian sponge cake layered with chocolate buttercream topped with caramel

daughter, Rebecca. These were my friends. I used to go to their store with Mother to buy materials for our Easter and Christmas outfits— striped cottons, flowered silks, smooth velvets were piled up high on the shelves. Mr. Schreiber used to joke with Mother. Mrs. Schreiber would invite me into the back room to have tea and a slice of bread and to talk to Rebecca, which I greatly enjoyed. I had long talks with Rebecca about life— she wanted to become a doctor and treat the poor of the town free. Her hair was light blonde and she had cornflower blue eyes; and because both her parents had dark hair and dark complexions, she was their little blonde angel, their fairy queen. They wished to protect her from the bad things of life; they loved her immensely.

Now she looked ill, her face very pale as she walked toward the wagon. Yet I didn't see her cry. Instead, I was the one who almost cried as our eyes met and she gazed at me in desperation. I wished with all my heart that I could do something for her. I wished that I could make her eyes look blue and happy again and not like dried-out wells (she must have been crying before). Although I didn't quite comprehend what was going on, my heart ached for her. I knew she was in danger. I approached from behind the statue and tried to get closer to the wagon into which the Jews were being herded, where Rebecca sat with her parents, along with dozens of other people who were packed in like sardines.

"Rebecca!" I shouted at last. "Rebecca!"

I couldn't get closer; a guard came and ordered me roughly away.

When I got to Grandma's house, all the relatives were already there for the birthday party. But it wasn't the gay gathering it usually was, but instead rather a somber affair. Everyone knew about the deporting of our city's Jews. We couldn't stop talking about it and felt frustrated that there was nothing we could do.

Later I went out to the garden with my cousins to play hide and seek. It was a nice afternoon, the sky as blue as Rebecca's eyes; yet I felt darkness all round me as if an enormous bird had blacked out the light, bringing death and destruction on its monstrous wings.

Chapter Two
THE STERNS

THE DAYS WERE STILL WARM and fragrant at the end of October, but the nights were cold because of the wind blowing from the hills, which surround the city like a fortress. Still, it was a typical small-town fall: the women cooking plum jam in huge iron kettles in the backyards of the houses, the yards full of shadows and falling leaves, the suffocating sweet smell of plum butter wrapping everything in a fragrant blanket.

In Saint George Meadow at the outskirts of the city, old peasant women sat on their porches in the sun, force-feeding the geese, stuffing them with grain. It was a noisy business, the women gossiping, the geese gaa-gaa-ing, and the wind singing like an old drunk soldier. The city was full of the shadows of fall, cumulus clouds swimming on the pale sky, slowly as in a dream. The flowers had withered in the gardens at the first touch of frost, yet it was still a beautiful, beautiful fall. I helped Mother carry her wicker basket to the local market, where we bought red winter apples and yellow pears, huge pitchers of sour cream, and homemade cheeses packed in coarse linen. We also bought goose liver, which Mother prepared at home with butter and milk and baked to a crispy perfection.

It was fun to go to the market where Mother knew all the farmers. They talked to her about their family problems. They, too, were deeply concerned about the deportation of the Jews, who were among their best customers. There were few families in the city that didn't have friends and relatives among the Jews— in our family, for example. Mother's sister, Bozsi, was married to one who I called Uncle Jeno. On the top of our piano we had a silver-framed, enlarged snapshot taken just before the wedding of the couple. They looked very happy standing there in the dark silence of the wood. They also looked very elegant, holding their silver-handled crops.

Klara and Tamas were born from that union and so they were my first cousins. They both had very dark hair and very blue eyes and an inborn elegance, which every one of the city's youth envied, including me, but in my case just a little bit. I was a small-town girl with a limited view because I hadn't traveled much, whereas Klara and Tamas were regular globetrotters. They felt at home in London and Paris, and even Lausanne where they had attended summer schools. Their father, Uncle Jeno, was rich, and influential in the town's politics. He owned several factories, a winery, and a lumber mill, a nice house in Esztergom, and a beautiful, magnificently furnished villa in Budapest on the Hills of Roses. Klara looked a little as one imagines Cleopatra, small and graceful and very chic, full of life and of sweet secrets, yet down to earth. She had beautiful manners and spoke several languages fluently, French, German, and English.

She had learned these languages from the many governesses who had come and gone in their home over the years. She was always the center of attention at family dinners, because she and Grandma spoke to each other either in German or French, which the rest of my cousins and I had just started to learn in school and so felt a little inferior.

Tamas and Klara had the mystery of wealth around them and the manners of the international "set." They had friends among the aristocracy all over the world, which they had met at school in Switzerland. At tea parties Klara was the star, and Tamas was greatly admired among the girls of the city. Along with the jealousy I felt, I also loved them with fervor, because they were so "different." Whenever I was invited to One of their houses, I came home dizzy with wonder at the intriguing combination of elegant people, beautifully decorated interiors, and gourmet food.

Mother and I often visited the Sterns (Aunt Bozsi, Uncle Jeno, Klara and Tamas) while in Budapest. After supper we would gather with them in the garden to enjoy the myriad lights of the city, which lie below, and listen to the gypsy music carried up the hill on the summer wind from the open-air restaurants.

We had not seen Tamas and Klara and their parents since the German invasion, and had been very anxious to find out what happened to them. Some of our friends who were able to communicate with their Jewish relatives in Budapest told us the terrible news that ghettos had been established in Budapest, while the Jews waited for further deportation. We also heard of the stringent measures taken by the Nazi government to isolate the Jews from the rest of the population, and of the cruel ways in which they carried them out.

Because of all this, Mother decided one day that we would go to Budapest to look up the Sterns. She was concerned about her sister, Aunt Bozsi, from whom she had not received a letter for quite some time.

We arrived at the Western Terminal on a Sunday morning, and then took the trolley from Pest to Buda to go to the Hills of Roses. On our way there we passed Dohany Street, a predominantly Jewish district, and noticed people emerging from their houses with huge yellow stars pinned to their chests. It was a shameful sight. I was shocked to see them like that, and felt very bad.

"The Jews," A middle-aged, red-faced man pointed at them with an implacable hatred in his eyes. He said it plain and bluntly, and made no further remarks. I shuddered at the tone of his voice, which was sharp as a razor's edge. Some of the passengers also looked at them with open hatred, others with pity, shaking their heads in disbelief. An old man who identified himself as a newspaper writer told us that the Jews were held to a strict curfew and could leave their houses only at certain hours.

The trolley crossed the Danube at the Margaret Bridge. The water of the river was dark, the color of lead. It began to rain. I was already worn out from emotion as we took the bus up to the Hills of Roses, a beautiful residential district with villas and elaborate gardens, and I was very disappointed when we found the gate of the Stern's villa locked. We went on ringing the bell for a long time. Finally, Teresa, their maid came out looking frightened. She told us that the family was not home. "They are hiding at the Rectory," she said. "At the Rectory of Monsignor Balmay. He is a good friend of mine. We were born in the same village and went to the same elementary school. I begged him to help the Sterns, to save them from deportation."

We took the bus and the trolley back again along the boulevards. It was very sad to see the once glittering capitol looking so grey and desolate in the rain, a sadness that penetrated the walls of the buildings, the asphalt of the streets. The doors of the Opera House and the National Theatre were closed, as were any stores owned by Jews. On Mezo Boulevard, where most of the sidewalk cafes were located, German officers were sitting, inside by the windows, as well as outside at the small white wrought-iron tables under the awning. The gay after-office crowd who used to chat and flirt there had simply vanished.

We found the Rectory at the end of a deserted street near an abandoned soccer field. It was an old building with shiny picture windows. Monsignor was working in his vegetable garden, his sleeves rolled up to his elbows. He greeted us with a friendly smile, and when we identified ourselves, he invited us inside. We followed him through the labyrinth of old brown rooms, as confusing as the catacombs in Rome, (I saw the catacombs when I was five years old and I still remembered the strong scent of myrrh, the same scent which emanated now from Monsignor's cassock, and from the dark hallways) and found our family and some other Jews sitting round a huge oak table eating potato paprikash. Uncle Jeno, Aunt Bozsi, Klara and other people were there: the widow of old Doctor Weiss; Mitzi and Samuel, who were both lawyers; Rachel and her two grandchildren. I was surprised to see that Klara's hair had been cut short and bleached a platinum blonde.

"She bleached her hair to make her look more like a gentile," whispered Aunt Bozsi.

They were very glad to see us, but told us that my cousin, Tamas, was missing. The Nazis on the street had picked him up a few days earlier.

"He complained of a headache. We waited for him all night to come back, in vain," wept his mother. Then the following morning a friend who worked the night shift at a nearby factory told them what had happened the previous night. He had witnessed two Nazi guards roughly grab the boy, beat him up and yell at him for not wearing the yellow star. Then he saw them drag him away. With the help of Monsignor, a few days later they were able to locate Tamas at the Eastern Railroad Terminal, about to be herded into a freight car with other Jews. They saw his pale and frightened face, yet they couldn't speak to him because of the guards who were all over.

They found that the train would leave soon, destination unknown, and so had a few hours to work on a rescue plan. They worked feverishly, went back to the city, purchased Nazi uniforms, and obtained some forged documents after much running around. They came back to the station, dressed like two high-ranking Nazi officers in their grey uniforms.

Close to the train. Monsignor picked out a guard who had the face of a donkey and intelligence to match, and handed him the documents, which stated that Tamas was wanted at the Nazi headquarters for interrogation. "The boy must come with us!" said Monsignor. "He is wanted for a number of criminal charges at headquarters. It is important! He must come with us! Espionage, and some money is involved. Gold Napoleons." The guard looked at the papers. The stamps seemed perfectly authentic. Within a few minutes he brought Tamas out from the wagon. He looked pale and sick and frightened and he was shaking. His father felt sick also to see his son looking so ill and frightened. At the same time he was intoxicated with happiness that his son was still alive. But he had to play a part: he slapped him in the face, calling him a son of a bitch, to keep the boy from giving them both away. "Where is the money?" he screamed. "Where are you hiding it?"

"Where is the jewelry, the stolen rings and bracelets?" cried Monsignor. To make such a commotion was their mistake. They overacted.

Upon hearing the noise another guard appeared. This one looked like a very, very tough guy, a born police hound. He knew right away that something was wrong. He pushed Tamas back to the wagon so violently that he fell on his knees. Then the guard grabbed the fake documents from Monsignor's hands. While he was studying them Monsignor and Uncle Jeno had to seize the opportunity to jump across the rails and escape. There was nothing else they could do. That was the end of the story, the story of their failed rescue attempt.

"There are some speculations that they will be taken to forced labor camps," moaned Uncle Jeno.

"Some of the poor souls threw pencil-written notes out of the window of the train, but when the notes were found, after a heavy rainstorm, the writing was illegible, the names smeared beyond recognition," cried Aunt Bozsi.

It was a terrible story and we all wept. The Sterns and everyone else praised Monsignor for his help. They told us that he had provided them with Christian birth certificates and some of them with jobs, such as clerks in the parish.

When we left the rectory, it was still raining, and the city was enveloped in grey mist all the way to the railroad station, as were our hearts.

"They are in God's hands," said Mother. "We must pray for them. That is all we can do."

Chapter Three
OCCUPATION RUSSIAN STYLE

CHRISTMAS of 1944 arrived with plenty of snow. The city looked silky and smooth with lilac and smoky reflections on the houses' roofs. The heavy snow muffled the noise of the streets, and the echo of the big bells of the Cathedral was intensified by the deep silence. I was walking toward Grandma's house with my parents to spend the Christmas there.

Everyone was already in the oval room when we got there (about fifty relatives). Ilona served big plates of fried fish as usual, and then homemade noodles sprinkled with crushed poppy seed. We all had mulled wine, sweetened with honey. Then we opened the presents, sang Christmas carols, and enjoyed the huge Christmas tree, the branches of the tree decorated with homemade candies and chocolate bonbons. The room was bathed in the aroma of the hot wine and the wax candles, vibrant with happy laughter.

Later on we walked together to the Midnight Mass along silent snow-covered roads. Inside the Basilica the marble pillars glowed with hundreds of candles. We joined in song with the choir of nuns, Mother, Father, Grandma and all. We prayed for everyone, including our Jewish relatives whom we hadn't heard from since our last visit— for Tamas and Klara, Aunt Bozsi and Uncle Jeno.

By now Budapest was surrounded by Soviet troops, and no one was allowed to enter or leave the city. There was no mail from there, no news, nothing.

On the first Sunday in January the first Soviet troops entered Esztergom. We were having an early dinner and Mother was serving the chicken soup. We heard noises outside, the sound of marching boots, of Russian speech. Father rushed out to the courtyard and locked the gate. Then he came back and drew the curtains across the windows. He looked deeply worried. The Soviets had a grim reputation everywhere they went, for looting and committing atrocities. We had heard terrible stories. In every village and city they entered, they forced the men against the wall and dragged the women from their hiding places and raped them. They would shoot anyone who resisted.

Father had prepared us carefully about what to do in case they came. Hearing the ominous sounds, he ordered Mother to go into the bedroom and disguise herself as an old woman, changing into one of Grandma's dresses, hiding her beautiful blonde hair under a dark peasant scarf.

I was told to run to the pantry at the back of the house. It was usually a lovely place to go, filled with canned goods, green figs, and sour cherries preserved in rum and syrup. A sea-green light came through the dark green glass window in the ceiling. I had hardly sat down on a half bag of dried nuts when I heard the first shots. Disobeying my father's orders, I ran through the rooms, and arrived in the dining room to find three Soviet soldiers standing in front of the gold-framed oil painting of Jesus Christ. One of them, a tall blonde man with light blue eyes, was still holding a gun, the other two, slanted-eyed Mongolians with dark complexions, stood by Father. I noticed with shock the bullet hole in the chest of Jesus. The blonde soldier turned in search of some other target. He put a bullet through the head of my china doll, who sat in her life-sized doll carriage. Father was watching the scene in suppressed anger. When Mother arrived dressed like an old woman, the soldier looked her up and down. Then his eyes fell on me, on my growing breasts, which showed through my sheer batiste blouse. Suddenly Mother pushed me out of the room. Then I saw her hurry into the kitchen from where she returned with a big plate of food. I heard her offering food and wine to the Russians. Afraid, as I stood in the darkness of the lobby, I went out to the garden, and climbed the bare branches of the elm tree. I sat there crying and trying not to think about the Russian soldiers and my china doll.

    That night after the Soviet soldiers came, my parents and I slept together in my parents' bedroom. Father double-locked the door, and he even wanted to push the heavy mahogany chest against it but Mother talked him out of that. I couldn't fall asleep. I heard the big clock striking midnight. After that I heard drunken singing coming from the direction of the dining room. A little later, I heard heavy footsteps right in front of our door. Someone began pounding on it. "Don't make a sound," whispered Father, "maybe he will go away." But the pounding became more insistent. Then a shot rang through the door but miraculously hit only the wall behind us.

"*Idi syuda, baryshnya*[†]*! Idi syuda!*" shouted a drunken voice outside. I ran to my parents' bed, weeping. Mother covered my mouth with her hands. When the pounding continued and became even more violent, she got out of bed and began to dress quickly. Father did the same. I begged them not to leave me alone.

"Both of you stay here," ordered Mother in a calm voice. "I'll go see what is going on."

Father protested and grabbed the hammer he kept by the bed, but Mother pushed him aside and hurried out. She feared for him; although Father was still very strong in spirit, his body was weakened by the progress of his disease. She knew he was certainly no match for a drunken soldier. I embraced him, seeking shelter in his arms. Through his shirt, I felt his skin feverishly hot. He was soaked with perspiration. For a while, we heard Mother's voice in the distance, talking calmly with the Soviet soldier, and then the soldier's drunken laugh. Then an uneasy stillness spread over the house for a long time. When she returned, her face looked strained. Her hair hung loose and damp around her face, her beautiful green eyes were sunken. The expression on her face resembled that of the Blessed Mother, the statue of the Pieta in the convent chapel.

"It is quiet out there now," she whispered. "We must try to get some sleep."

All night we huddled in a close embrace. In my half sleep, I heard Mother and Father weeping.

I woke up early and heard someone pounding on the front door, and recognized the voice of Tante Mariska who lived across the street.

---

† come here, woman

"We need a doctor in a hurry, we need your sweet Mama," she pleaded as I let her in. She told us that during the night four Soviet soldiers had entered her house, where the first floor was rented to Bela and Zsofi, an elderly couple. Zsofi was in the kitchen preparing supper when the soldiers came, her husband Bela taking a nap in the bedroom. He woke up when he heard his wife screaming, but couldn't help her as the soldiers dragged her away. He tried, but the soldiers pushed him down the cellar and locked the door. Next morning, when Zsofi was released and came home, she found her husband in the cellar hanging from a rope.

"She is still in shock," cried Tante Mariska.

I watched as Mother carrying the medical kit followed her across the street. I thought that in all my life I have never seen anyone as beautiful as my mother. A ray of sunshine lit up her blonde bun.

The early afternoon when Bela was buried was lime green. Hundreds of people went to the cemetery to say goodbye to him. They covered his grave with flowers and laid the national flag on it. Two Soviet tanks circled the cemetery all through the ceremony, but the burial ended without incident.

In the weeks following the Soviet occupation, the Red soldiers in our city raped hundreds of women, yet no one dared report any atrocities. The occupation of the country was called "Liberation" and the Soviet soldiers were "Heros"; a complaint against them would be considered a crime, punishable by imprisonment. The roads of our city swarmed with Soviet armored cars, and big-breasted Mongolian army policewomen stood at the intersections where Hungarian policemen used to stand, directing the traffic. From then on, the city changed hands again and again, depending on who won on the battlefields, the Germans or the Soviets. German and Soviet soldiers came and went, leaving the shelves in the stores empty. I stayed at home and had no choice but to listen to the barking of the cannon that shattered our windows.

By the end of May, all was quiet at the front. The Germans had been defeated; the Red Army occupied every area of Hungarian soil.

* * *

One day I set out for Grandma's house, treading the deserted streets under the cold spring sunshine. The war was over. The invasion of the Germans, the fighting against the Soviets, the bombings by the American warplanes had ended, but left the city and us the worse for wear. Most of the houses were deserted. The antique furniture, Bohemian crystal chandeliers, oil paintings, and Meissen chinaware had been hauled away, taken to the U.S.S.R. on trucks and freight cars.

Thank God that the Basilica still stands, I thought. Its gigantic white and pink marble pillars still glowed in the sun, a symbol of a spiritual message, and the sounds of its big bells echoed across the valleys.

Thirty-six of us waited in the oval room for Grandma who was celebrating her seventy-sixth birthday. Her children and her grandchildren awaited her eagerly, aunts, uncles and all. Before my time, I was told, over a hundred relatives would gather here to celebrate her birthday. As the years went by they became less in number. I assumed they had all gone to heaven. Except perhaps one, my Aunt Irene, for whose peace of soul and salvation I was taught to recite the rosary five times a week at home with Grandma, and once each Sunday during the afternoon service at Watertown Church.

Aunt Irene had been Grandma's youngest daughter. I heard her story on a rainy day in the maids' quarters, from our old maid Lina who had the face of a kind witch. According to her, Irene was always a little eccentric. She not only spoke German and French and a little Latin, but she played the piano every night, Chopin and Ravel and Beethoven, to the children, before they fell asleep. She was a fragile and sentimental soul, too much in love with her philandering husband.

Erno, her husband, was a captain in the Royal Army. He was a handsome man who had many mistresses, even ladies from the upper class, and he frequently visited the maids' quarters in his own house for that same purpose. Knowing all that for a number of years, Irene wept in secret, in her sewing room, to which she withdrew at dusk. She would sit crying while the faint scent of gardenias and camellias drifted through the windows, the scents of spring and summer and fall making her heart ache. Nevertheless, she kept the family together for the children's sake until, one November on All Souls' Day.

It was a cold and windy day. Her husband was away on his yearly maneuvers in the mountains. The young maid, Lea, threw up three times during breakfast, as she served the tea. Irene had a long talk with her afterwards. "It is your husband's fault Madame," said the maid, "that I am pregnant. It is Madame's husband who forced his way to my room every night!" At five o'clock that afternoon, as on All Souls' Day every year, Irene went to the cemetery. She lit twenty white and twenty yellow candles in the family vault. Then she said her prayers for the family's dead members. Many people were in the cemetery that day. A number of them spoke to her and remembered years later how beautiful she looked with her pale blonde hair glistening in the candlelight.

"But when she came home," said the old maid Lina, "she wouldn't touch the cup of chamomile tea I brought her. She kept to her room and didn't even come out to kiss the children in the nursery."

The following day the maid's father came up from the village and took her home, cursing the inhabitants of the house. That same day Irene had risen early. She wore a white crisp cotton dress under her fur coat and had pinned a white chrysanthemum in her hair. Then, holding a small red-leather book in her hand, she left the house.

Swiftly, she walked to the railroad station. When the morning express from Budapest approached the platform, she threw herself onto the railroad tracks. Her head was cut off instantly. In her book she had written a message to her mother, yet Grandma has never shown the message to anyone, not even to Irene's husband.

* * *

Grandma is taking her time today; people are getting impatient. Ilona closes the French windows to keep the furious spring wind out. The old maid, Lina, brings in fragrant yellow and purple *babarózsa*‡ bouquet sent to Grandma by her admirers. I don't know why but the musty odor and the

---

‡ peony

choking dampness of the room makes me think about death. The dead ones, where do they go? Does my Father still exist somewhere? Is he able to see me now? He should be here with us today. I would give my soul to bring him back.

Father died at home on an exquisite spring day while the lilies and purple violets smelled sweet in our garden, and his soul went to heaven with the joyous singing of the birds. I watched while Mother closed his eyes, washed his body, and dressed him in his best. She folded his arms over his chest and then she went to the piano and played Rachmaninoff's "Prelude in C-sharp minor", his favorite composition. Mother explained to me that this had been by agreement between them. While we both cried because of the mysterious beauty of the music and because our loved one had left us, she told me the story behind Rachmaninoff's composition of the prelude. It was written in memory of his best friend who was buried while only apparently dead. When he was later exhumed, it was discovered that he had been buried alive. She should not have told me that I was haunted for years, imagining that Father had also been buried alive.

Now death has become a common topic. Most people have someone missing in action. Even the letters from the prisoners of war are full of anguish on the rare occasions they reach us from Kharkov or Ivanova. Our life is filled with death and anxiety and sadness.

Everyone feels relieved when Grandma finally appears, heralded by her favorite perfume, herself clad in black silk and lace, her thin cheeks faintly rouged and powdered.

Dinner is served on the porch under the pink blossoms of oleander trees. The maids bring in the goulash.

Uncle Demeter is seated next to me. Suddenly, he begins to reminisce about the better days they'd all known in the past:

> Your Grandma was always fond of the Dionysian pleasures of the table, but nowadays we only have soup. I shall never forget a fabulous feast served on one of her birthdays. Was it before the war? I don't remember now. But there were capon sprinkled with raisins, lamb fillets cooked in almond milk, a whole tongue in a fruit puree, olives, blood sausages, peacock with gravy, spiced ham, and boiled pig's head, almond- stuffed chickens, pomegranates, chestnuts cooked in heavy cream, sugared almonds, strudel made with dilled cottage cheese. I remember we drank brandy before the soup, and wine, white wine, after the fish. It breaks my heart that in your Grandma's wine cellar, the barrels are now empty. That happened on the first day of the Soviet invasion. I'll never forget that day.
>
> The Red Army opened all the casks, then they drank all the wine they could, and the rest they poured on the ground. Wine was flowing on the streets those days.

He shouldn't be saying these things. It affects the mood of the guests; their gloomy thoughts become almost visible in the haunted air.

But with good timing, at absolutely the right psychological moment, liquor is served on Grandma's orders. But instead of crystal goblets as of old, it is served in ordinary thick glasses.

The crystal went when the victorious Red Army marched across the town and were billeted in the homes of citizens. There were seventeen at Grandma's house, among them Captain Misha. He was a little bohemian, a very unusual trait in Soviet officers. He was also a gentleman. By his orders, his Uzbekhian orderly would bring food for Grandma, sugar and eggs, live rabbits and chickens, which of course he probably commandeered from one of the neighbors.

One day Captain Misha asked Grandma to lend him her small dining room in order to give a party for a few high-ranking comrades, just arrived from the U.S.S.R. Grandma knew she must not refuse his request. There were rumors of shooting incidents in the city when the owners of the houses denied the requests of the Soviet officers quartered in their homes.

The party was a success. The comrades had a great time. They ate and drank and sang Russian songs, which had the effect of putting them in a nostalgic mood. They drank more vodka, they sang more songs, and around midnight the pain in their Asiatic souls grew unbearable. Some of them were weeping. To ease the pain, Misha began shooting the lovely miniatures on the wall mounted in Blondell frames. Then he began to aim at the Bohemian crystal glasses on the table.

I have heard the story before and it does not affect me anymore. I take a few sips from Uncle Demeter's grog, which is made of mulled wine spiced with acacia honey and cloves. It tastes good. I feel intoxicated. My cousin Evi, who has lived with Grandma since her mother Irene's death, and

I excuse ourselves from table to go to the hanging garden. To get there we have to cross the second courtyard filled with asparagus plumosus in large wooden barrels, then across another porch bright with geraniums.

The hanging garden is located at the side of the house where the hill starts. There is a rock wall with a long ladder in front of it, which one must climb up. Then one must jump onto the tin roof, which is on a level with the room under the eaves. From there you can look down on the entire city, with the Danube in the center, a meandering pink ribbon against the orange glow of the sunset. Just now the evening air is fresh and cool. I feel as though I am sitting inside a soft balloon, safe from the disturbing world.

Evi breaks the silence. "Tomorrow, I am going out with a Soviet officer," she whispers, searching my face for a reaction. "Did you hear me? I have a date with a Russian. Go and tell Grandma. She will faint."

"I won't tell," I whisper back.

"Yes you will," she jeers. "And I don't care!" She leaves with a coquettish wiggle of her fifteen-year-old, melon-shaped buttocks, holding her small head exactly as her mother used to, with a kind of a strange mixture of shyness and pertness.

I thought about Evi after she left. I was fond of her and hoped that she wouldn't get into trouble dating a Russian, like the neighbor's daughter, Annuska, who became pregnant by a Red soldier. I had heard the story at dinnertime last Sunday when the same crowd of relatives gathered here for stuffed cabbage. I understood every word although the conversation was held in German and in French so that the children round the table wouldn't understand the shameful story of Annuska and her lover.

I had studied both languages in school and was all ears to find out about any forbidden topic. Besides, it wasn't difficult to put two and two together. I had seen Annuska with my own eyes. She liked to sit in her garden under a tree, reading with a dreamy expression on her face, dressed in a soft white tunic such as virgins wear in the Greek mythology books. I noticed however that underneath her soft white tunic she was getting bigger and bigger. It would be interesting to find out more about her, I thought, about the piquant details of her love affair which made everyone's face flush, (and excited little laughs would circle in the air), with the exception of Grandma who was a calm as usual.

"*C'est la vie*," she said. "The victorious army has always left its mark on the female portion of a conquered population, during most of the wars in the history of mankind. It isn't worth getting excited about it."

"Who did it? For what reason?" I heard Uncle Demeter asking. He sat at the far end of the table and was deaf as a post. And he also looked a little tipsy, having had too much mulled wine.

Then I heard Uncle Karsci say that on his last trip to Vienna, he had noticed blonde Frauleins pushing baby carriages with lovely mulatto kids in them on the Graben. "Souvenirs from the American Army in World War II," he said.

Lina, the old maid who sat with us at the dinner table, was silently pondering the topic, her wrinkled old face looking wise and about a thousand years old.

"Foolish, not very smart," she declared later.

"Who is a fool? Are you talking about me again?" Uncle Demeter shouted from the far end.

"It is very foolish," Lina continued, "doing things like that, sleeping with the enemy while there are 'professionals' in our city, the girls on Almos Street. Just as in most of the cultures of the world, we have our professionals. Then why must girls from good families sleep with the Russians, I ask myself?"

She pronounced her words very slowly so that everyone around the table would understand despite her peasant accent.

"In the case of Annuska, love is the name of the game," said Aunt Nesta who has never married. She looked pale, almost envious, and she would have liked to hear more detail. "The girl was in love and vice versa," she said. Seeing that she wanted to continue the topic Grandma interrupted her. "Who wants to play canasta?" she asked, and she gave orders to the maids to bring tea and bread to the oval room.

"Love shmuv! It is a good excuse," I heard Lina mutter to herself as she left the table, walking with energetic steps and now looking years younger and more invigorated. The old tired faces of my uncles and aunts had also undergone a remarkable transformation, talking about Annuska and the Russian. Wrinkles seemed to smooth out, colorless eyes sparkle, waxy and transparent skins turn the color of dying roses. It was heartwarming to talk about love of any kind; it brought back old memories.

"The girls on Almos Street are finished," declared Uncle Karcsi. "Soon the red-light district in our city will be demolished. The girls will be trained to be taxi drivers and other things. Communism doesn't tolerate prostitution. There are no pleasure districts in the Soviet Union."

I had known about the girls on Almos Street for a long time. I loved to walk on the dark, narrow streets where their small houses stood isolated. In fact, I made sure to pass through the district every time I went to Grandma's house. There was a girl named Ibi, whom I liked particularly. She always greeted me with a friendly smile. She had thick, sensual lips, and small, pearly, crooked teeth. She never failed to smile at me, and I returned her smile. I inhaled the strange mixture of odors, which emanated from the houses: face powder, cheap perfume, a long, hot summer, potato paprikash and garlic. And I loved the magenta-colored velvet ribbon in Ibi's hair, which she sometimes changed to a pale blue silk, according to the weather and her mood. She wore black skirts and blouses, and she always looked a little secretive, as if she possessed something precious. The girls sat on the long wooden benches at the front of their house waiting for something, I thought, enjoying their strong cigarettes, their chain-smoking, and their afternoon gossip. Their clothes were slightly provocative. Other than that they looked just like any other women in our city

I never mentioned my visits to the red-light district to Mother or to Grandma, and I didn't quite understand my fascination with those back streets. Yet my visits went on until Uncle Karcsi's prediction came true and the district was demolished. Then I missed the setup, its strangeness and its exoticism, and I felt that our town was no longer such an interesting place.

I remember that day and conversation well, the topic of love has always fascinated me. I think about love and Annuska all the time.

I don't know much about the Soviet Union, our new overlord. I have seen the snapshots the Soviet soldiers showed us, but that's all. In those pictures there are big-breasted *baryshnya* dressed in dark babushkas, usually standing in front of shabby log cabins. There are long, empty streets covered with piles of snow, barren streets with onion-domed churches in the background, and an over-all sadness on everything.

I like to sit here on the roof, reflecting, thinking about Evi and Annuska and the Russians and everything. But there is a chill in the air now; a wind sweeps over the shrubs and trees, a cold wind coming from the direction of the hills. I take a last look at the wavering masses of blue hills both near and at a distance, and at the huge marble pillars of the Basilica bathed now in the sepia brown of approaching evening.

I wonder if the guests are already dancing to the tunes of *csárdás*[§] in the oval room. I should join them. One last glance down at the streets below and I notice something interesting. I see a carriage approaching, from the direction of Saint Margit Street, drawn by one horse. Then I notice that people are coming out of the houses and following the carriage. They are all coming toward Grandma's house, adults and children, and the carriage drawn by one horse.

I run through the weeds, go down the ladder, arrive at the porch with palpitating heart, just in time to hear the doorbell ring.

Through the glass door of the oval room, I see the servants turning on the electric lamps, and people gathering around the piano. Aunt Katinka is sitting in front of it, her face flushed with excitement. Grandma is playing cards at the far end of the veranda that overlooks the gates, with uncles and aunts whose faces are as red as the geraniums, which are all over the place. Now everyone's head turns toward the house door, as if they were spectators at a tennis match. They are listening to the house bells.

---

§ a Hungarian dance

I am the first one to step outside; others follow right behind me, even Grandma. There is a carriage in front of the house. A woman dressed in shabby clothes holds the reins; another lies on the hay inside the wagon. I recognize her instantly. She is my cousin, Ester, who fled from town with her husband when the Soviets invaded Hungary and the Hungarian Army retreated into Austria, pursued by T-34 Soviet tanks. Her husband, Sandor, was an officer in the Army. I remember him only faintly, since I wasn't at their wedding, which was held in Watertown, in 1944.

Everyone stands speechless now in front of the wagon. Because today is Saturday, Didi, the gypsy woman has arrived with her seven children, to be fed with the leftover food. She grabs Ester's hands and showers them with kisses, tears flowing down her brown Indian face. And the town's fool, Ethel, arrives, clinging to a lamppost, a childish joy on her withered face, laughing hysterically, repeating over and over: "She is baaack, little Ester is back in town, baaaack, baaaack, baaaack."

Then she runs down the street, her hair flying. She cries and she laughs, and she looks like a rag doll in her long, old-fashioned clothes.

When we bring Ester back to the house, the rooms come alive with laughter and with joy. There is a big commotion; everyone wants to do something for her. Lina, the old maid, brings camphor and chamomile tea, while Ilona, the young one, brings apricot liquor.

Someone calls Doctor Emmanuel on the phone, and he arrives shortly in his black lacquered coach. "We will bring her back to life," he says, reassuringly.

I hope he knows how to revive her. He was the one who brought her into the world twenty-five years ago, on a hot, windless summer day, he has told me. "She was tiny like a snowflake, fragile like the mimosa flower in your Grandma's garden, wholesome like a home-baked bread," says old Doctor Emmanuel. "She was loud and aggressive, even when she was a tiny baby. Don't you worry, she possesses all the necessary qualities to help her to recover."

I pray to God that he is right. She looks deathly ill right now.

Chapter Four
THE STORY OF ESTER

ESTER CAME BACK HOME riddled with ailments, and I often visited her at Grandma's house, where she was put up in the room under the eaves. To cure these ailments she was given hearty beef soups and goose liver, selected with care by Grandma at the market then baked to perfection in milk and butter. She stayed in bed most of the time reading Gone With The Wind, reading it over and over until she knew each sentence by heart. Slowly, she got better, and I in the meantime felt bored to death with the dullness of my life. Ester had gone through adventures, had something to remember, but what did I have? I had to take exams during those school years and attend seminars to study the ideology of Stalin and Lenin, as was mandated by the newly organized school system, which didn't seem to me to lead me anywhere in particular. In my free time I loafed in the sun, waiting for my mother to return from the hospital where she was spending more and more time since Father's death, while I stayed lonely in our long gray house.

When Ester was feeling good, she and I would lean out of the window of her room watching the passersby and talking about life before the war.

"Remember how young and carefree we were?" she would ask. We talked of Saint Stephen's Day and the Pilgrimage to the Basilica, with nostalgia. The night before, the peasants would arrive from the villages, sleeping on their wagons or on blankets thrown on the sidewalk, in order to be in time for the event next morning. Then they would dress up in all their colors: the women's skirts embroidered with cornflower blue and saffron yellow and poppy red, the men in crisp white shirts and black boots so shiny that the sky seemed to be reflected on them. The miners arrived from the mining villages dressed in black velvet. The whole town joined the procession, following the Bishop who carried the Sacrament, young girls walking before him in their white lace dresses and veils, and scattering freshly cut grass and rose petals from wicker baskets. The fragrance of the flowers and of the wax candles that stood lighted on the windowsill filled the air and the murmur of ancient prayers. After the procession we all went to the fair, booths laden with figurines of blue-eyed Madonnas, with sacred candles, and with Turkish delight. The big bells of the Basilica echoed constantly across the rolling hills, and the aroma of cinnamon and other spices drifted from the houses of the gingerbread makers, the smell of sausages from the open-air kitchens. "Nowadays everything has a horrid taste of ashes," I said to Ester. "The Communists have banned all gatherings. Instead of Saint Stephen's Day, for example, we have to celebrate the birthdays of Stalin and Lenin, and applaud enthusiastically. We have to carry red flags, and shout "Down with the American Imperialists!"

We decided to start writing a book, to keep our spirits up, a book about the adventures of Ester's life, which would start with her wedding in 1944, when the Red Army had already broken through the Carpathian Mountains into Transylvania, our Eastern province. Her fiancé Sandor (he looked like Tyrone Power) was there with his regiment fighting against the Soviets. He was granted a leave just long enough for the wedding in Watertown. When he and Ester emerged from the church and walked under the gleaming swords held over their heads by fellow officers, Ester had tripped on her long veil. "Bad omen," people whispered. After the reception the couple left by train to Gegled, a military center in which Sandor was living near the old freight station, whose empty warehouses and motionless machines now lay dreaming in the darkness. They arrived in the middle of the night, to see his house lit up by brilliant moonlight. Inside, his orderly awaited them with a bottle of Tokay, and with hot chicken soup. The new husband embraced his wife, kissing her flaxen hair and passionate blue eyes, and the whole room filled with their mutual desire. Suddenly, a ghastly shriek of sirens tore the air. An air raid was on! Ester and Sandor had to leave the house in a hurry and run to a nearby stubble field where they crouched through the night, listening to the hissing of bombs and watching with terror the scarlet flames as the city burned. The stubble field was at a distance from the house and relatively safe from the bombs, but when they went home around dawn, they had to jump over craters and burning timbers and rubble where houses had once stood. They were too tired to make love on this first day of their honeymoon and soon Sandor had to return to the battlefield, leaving Ester alone. She missed her husband and was afraid in the lonely house where silence reigned, and only the harsh fall wind could be heard outside the closed window. Sometimes she would take walks in the nearby acacia forest but usually she just sat on the blue velvet chaise lounge with a faraway look in her eyes. At night she left the light on.

One night Ester woke up drenched in perspiration. She was astonished to hear the cries of people she thought she was hearing in her dream. She opened the window and in the darkness saw a group of people standing across the field and heard someone begging for water. She went out, crossed the road and saw armed guards standing by the group, one of them beating an old man. "Get up and go, you fucking Jew!" he shouted. An ice-cold hand seemed to grab Ester by the throat. The thought of her cousins, Tamas and Klara flashed through her mind. The old man continued to stretch out his arms, begging for water. The guard threatened her with the butt of his rifle, when she offered to fetch water for the old man. When the group was finally driven away, she returned to the house and felt sick, not understanding what could be happening. The next day in the local market when she went to buy food she heard about deportation of the Jews. She was told that the Nazis were taking advantage of the fact that the nation was busy fighting against the invading Soviet forces, and they had decided to deport the Jews.

Ester passed lonely days and lonely nights without Sandor. Then on a cold spring night when she thought her loneliness had lasted too long to bear, he came back. He was with the retreating Hungarian Army, and told her that Budapest had fallen after two months of siege, and the city left in ruins. He had come to pick her up so that they could together join the convoy of other officers and soldiers and their families, who were leaving Hungary by Division orders. All the way to Austria their convoy was to be harassed and pursued by Russian tanks. It had been a dangerous journey, yet she was thrilled to be reunited with her husband.

They finally reached an Austrian farmhouse that looked out on three linden trees and stood on a small hill. The owners allowed them to spend the night in the barn. There Ester and Sandor made love for the first time, under the rough military blanket, while an enchanting melody of guitars floated up from the nearby valley, and the linden trees gave off their spring fragrance, decayed yet sweet. She could hear the nostalgic singing of other troopers, the moans of other lovers from other dark corners, and her heart swelled with happiness. The convoy was on the road for a week, sleeping at various farmhouses, on trucks or sometimes on the sidewalk, when a farmer didn't welcome them to his house. In the morning, they would wash in spring water, or in a nearby brook.

On April 28th, the convoyed group reached Steier, an industrial city on the banks of the River Steier, and there they learned that the war was over. Along the valley they saw for the first time American tanks, which they stared at in curiosity. Then a few hours later, the Division was ordered to start back for Hungary, and they turned wearily around, to retrace their way home. They passed the vestiges of recent battles, burned-out German and Russian tanks, dead soldiers who lay on the new grass and stared at the sky with marbled eyes. They came upon a clear brook where a handwritten warning was pinned upon a small bridge: "Do not cross. Cholera epidemic." They crossed it anyway. The village looked beautiful with its blossoming young trees and lovely old houses, but fumes of sickness hung in the air like a shroud.

After leaving the streets of the deserted village, they passed a few armed Soviet soldiers with machine guns raised, guarding a crossroad. They were ordered to put down their weapons and separate into two lines, women to the left, men to the right. The women clung together like frightened birds, as their men were led away to the sound of harsh Soviet voices.

After a while Ester left the group of women and went down to the river alone. She sat for a long time listening to the irregular beat of her heart. Night came, and although physically and mentally exhausted, she couldn't sleep. She laid there, her eyes fixed on the ripples of the river; when dawn came, she was still motionless. "This is death," she thought, "and I am not going to struggle against it." She wasn't sure if the woman coming toward her through the meadow was real or an apparition.

As the woman came closer, Ester recognized her. It was Ida, the wife of one of Sandor's fellow officers.

"I've found a place where I think we can steal a horse and a wagon," she said in a low whisper.

Together the two women crept through the meadow where a farm stood hidden behind a hedge. A dimly lit stable was at the corner of the house, and the warmth and smell of horses drifted through the open door.

* * *

We had just gotten that far with Ester's story when she began to complain that she had "writer's block." This stopped us from writing for almost another year. "It is too painful to remember," she would say. "I don't know if my husband is dead or alive." Although she was far from invulnerable, I had never seen her cry. There was strong pride in her, characteristic of our family. The more we suffered, the more rebellious and bold we became; suffering had taught us how to wait for better days.

Suffering had taught us how to lose and how to recover from loss, how to hang onto life, that fickle creature.

* * *

In the summer of 1949, it didn't rain for a whole month. The gardens in the city took on a faint yellowish color, the bushes withered, and the petals of the flowers drooped as if they were dying. The water of the Danube sank low, so low that it was impossible to hold the usual yearly high school boat race. The streets around the Bishop's Palace were covered with amber-colored dust, which the strong, dry wind easily stirred up. Everyone closed the windows of their homes, tightly, but uselessly. The dust stole through the windows and into the rooms while furious maids flicked their dust cloths at all hours of the day.

Even the city fell under the heat spell, the air became stale and tasted like sugar, the sidewalks by the railroad station gray from the streams of smoke. The asphalt ribbon breaks off sharp from the heat; old women's faces gleam with a pinkish pallor as they hurry to church; street urchins became like little monsters that throw burrs at people that stick to their backs.

I am at Grandma's house, wilted by the heat and drinking one glass of tepid water after another when Ester comes in from the garden with a glowing face, holding a cable in her hand. "From the Red Cross," she cries. "Good news."

The cable from the Red Cross in Geneva informs her that Sandor is alive and about to be shipped home from Siberia. We spend the next week rejoicing while we clean house and buy new pillows and sheets from a woman in the neighborhood who makes her living embroidering linens.

We pick the ripe currants in the hanging garden and soak them in a barrel to ferment them for wine. Then we gather a basket of gooseberries from which Ester makes a special sauce, Sandor's favorite. After we have finished with all this activity, she becomes depressed. When I question her, she blames it on the weather. To keep up her spirits, I take her to the local patisserie, where the red velvet curtains, the white-and-gold baroque furniture, and the soft music of the Coppélia Waltz coming from the radio make her relax. We order hot-chocolates with whipped cream. Then she begins to reminisce, taking me back with her to the roads of Austria when she and Ida were making their way back home on the wagon.

It did her good to talk about it. She told me how they drove the wagon across the vast rye and wheat fields, beneath the cruel summer sky, avoiding the main roads at all cost, because they knew the Soviet Army used those to pull their division out of Austria at the conclusion of the war. The two women were exhausted, hungry, and thirsty, and were not at all sure of the roads they drove on. They drove during the day and at sundown tried to find shelter of some kind. If a farmer was in a good mood, he would let them sleep in the stable, but most of the time they slept on top of the wagon. They often heard shooting and the drunken singing of Soviet soldiers in the distance, or the screams of women who were being dragged away. They were hungry and cold and frightened in the swampy odor of the strange country.

On the third day of their journey they must have drunk contaminated water for they became sick, feeling dehydrated and dizzy. Ester thought that she had lost her senses and that traveling on those lonely roads in the wagon was only happening in a nightmare. The two women often had to stop to empty their bowels in the fields where they squatted and moaned from pain. Once Ester returned to the wagon screaming, "There is a dead woman lying back there."

The two women dragged themselves back to the field where the dead woman lay between the rows of grain, naked and bathed in the ray of sinking sun. They laid a wild flower on her. Then the smell of dried blood and urine sickened them and they dragged themselves back to the wagon.

That same night they got lost on the roads and panicked. They met an old peasant woman who put them in the right direction and when they finally reached the Hungarian border they found an impromptu official board of inquiry waiting. Russian and Hungarian soldiers were sitting round an old kitchen table at the side of the dirt road and checking the people who wanted to reenter Hungary. Large numbers of haggard, disheveled people were arriving in wagons, in military vehicles, and on foot.

Ester and Ida looked seriously sick and the Communist officer, yawning and running his fingers through his hair, let them go without much questioning. He was probably tired, too. Then in about an hour the two women reached the first Hungarian village. Through the open door of a thatched cottage, they saw an old woman squatting on the dirt floor sorting beans into a huge iron pot, yellow-gold baby chickens running in and out and around her legs. She invited them in.

When the farm family came home from the fields, they invited Ester and Ida to stay for supper. The bottle of white Riesling, which the farmer brought up from the cellar, was good and strong. He drank a lot and the wine loosened his tongue. He spoke about an open-air camp he had noticed some time ago at the other end of the village. "It is packed with war prisoners!" he said.

Hearing what he said Ester's heart skipped a beat. Maybe Sandor is among the prisoners, she thought. The farmer also mentioned a Soviet captain, who, according to rumor, was of Hungarian descent and had helped some of the prisoners to freedom. "He lives near the camp," said the farmer.

The women wasted no time early next morning setting out for the camp. The air was fragrant and cool, yet Ester was bathed in perspiration. Her heart contracted when she saw the camp under the birch trees, an elevated platform packed with prisoners with shaved heads. Armed Soviet soldiers stood by the fence.

Upon the advice of the farmer, she had brought a bottle of wine and she now offered it to the guard who approached her. He snatched it and walked swiftly away. She moved closer to the fence, searching among the unshaved faces, and suddenly saw Sandor. He stood right there; his dark, sad eyes stared at her as if all feeling had been drained from them. They looked at each other silently, knowing that to talk would be forbidden.

"They can't take him away from me," Ester thought. "Not this time."

At that moment some more guards arrived and tried to chase the women away, shooting into the air. Ester ran toward the back of the camp where she saw some wooden bungalows standing under the trees. She came upon a young Soviet officer and asked him about Captain Rostoff, whose name she had learned from the farmer.

He led her to one of the small bungalows, where inside a darkened room she found the captain lying on a cot, his face flushed with fever and looking quite ill. She begged him to do something for her husband.

He said she had come too late. "I am sick," he said, "Malaria. I have had a recurrence of malaria, and am also under house arrest." He said he was under house arrest because his superiors found out that he had been rescuing prisoners. He urged Ester to leave.

She did so very reluctantly and was immediately escorted out by two armed guards. She was then led to a barn which had been converted into an office, and there sat half a dozen high-ranking Soviet officers behind a long kitchen table, waiting.

Through an interpreter, a red-faced officer inquired the name of the person who knew about Captain Rostoff. When she repeatedly refused to reveal the farmer's name, the officer rose and screamed at her, his face even redder with anger, shouting in Russian. "You must leave the village at once or you will be deported to the U.S.S.R.," warned the interpreter.

She wouldn't have minded being deported to the U.S.S.R. along with her husband, but she was roughly pushed out of the barn by the armed guards. By now the open-air camp was deserted and when she turned back to have a last glance, only the wind was whistling over the fields.

* * *

When Sandor came back from Siberia, he looked at once pale and bloated, not all skin and bone as one would have expected. We learned that he had spent the last weeks in a special rehabilitation camp before being sent home. He was in a camp in Latvia, and fed sugar and bread and sugar water in order to put on weight. This was an order of the Swiss Red Cross, who insisted the Soviets do something about their prisoners, who were too weak to endure the long train journey back to Hungary from the U.S.S.R.

The loving care he got from us, soon brought back his good looks, but he was like a bottomless pit, swallowing enormous amounts of food. He also had developed some personality changes. He never talked of his ordeal. It had begun on the freight train, which took them to Russia, where they were packed so tightly that they had to sleep on top of each other and urinate and defecate through a hole cut in the train floor. He never once referred to the endless days and frozen nights in the primitive barracks somewhere in Siberia, where many of the prisoners died; or to the rats or to the human feces scattered all over until the prisoners dug their own outhouse in the frozen earth. Of all this we heard from Viola whose husband returned at the same time as Sandor.

Now Ester and Sandor spent most of their time in the room under the eaves playing the piano, always the same piece, Ravel's Boléro. I don't know if Ester is satisfied with her life now. I don't know. I only hope to God that she is.

Chapter Five
LIFE AFTER THE INVASION

THE PRESENCE OF THE RED ARMY was a drag almost unbearable in a small town like Esztergom. The Hungarian army simply vanished from the red brick barracks on Main Street to be replaced by Soviet soldiers, who walked in groups behind the iron fence and who appeared tense and suspicious of everything. Once the army was established, their families began to arrive: fair-haired children with turned-up noses, and big-breasted women dressed in outdated clothes in drab colors and of cheap material. They were eager to be a part of the sophisticated life of Western Europe.

The Soviets had a store on Main Street that was stocked with merchandise unavailable to Hungarians, such as bananas and oranges, chocolate, and cocoa, coffee and other imported goods. Their presence didn't bother me, but the old people like Grandma found the change hard to accept. Their life had altered as drastically as if a light had been extinguished.

At night, the familiar crowd was missing from the street by the Danube and from under the shade trees where they used to sit and gossip after the evening meal. The new members of the Party sent from Budapest now occupied the city exclusively, discussing Stalin and Benin and the ideology of Communism.

The steamboats on the Danube, loaded of old with tourists, ceased to run. As a result, Grandma's business suffered and the restaurant went bankrupt. Her house remained filled with impoverished relatives for whom she did everything, including feeding them. Ester and Sandor still lived in the room under the eaves, and a few old aunts and uncles occupied various other rooms. She struggled to provide them with food, which was scarce and expensive as most of the harvest and the livestock was sent to the U.S.S.R. and left only the barest necessities to the Hungarians.

Grandma worked very hard. Although she never complained, she began to lose her rugged and healthy appearance, and one night she died unexpectedly in her sleep. Her limp yet rigid body was found in her dark, rose water and powder-smelling room by Aunt Katinka, her second daughter, who was a divorcee and also lived in the house. Grandma was laid out in the oval room for three days, looking fragile and shriveled on the black catafalque. I stood by her and talked to her quietly, while the throngs of relatives sobbed there behind their black veils. It seemed as though they sobbed to the rhythm of the flickering candlelight. The maids kept opening and closing the windows— to allow the fresh air in and to keep out the sickening sweet smell of death, while everyone just stood by the catafalque and sobbed and sobbed and cried aloud.

One month after the burial, the restaurant and the house were put up for auction. I happened to be there that day and I watched the bidding until the house was virtually stripped, only the odor of spicy food and beer and wine remained, ingrained in the walls.

No one dared to bid for the shiny black baby-grand piano, which stood below the poetic bronze branches of a lamp. No one dared to make an offer, because of Aunt Katinka, who stood in front of it like a Cerberus. People still remembered her summer night concerts, the sweet variegated melodies drifting through her windows. People still remembered.

After the auction I went to the cemetery to visit Grandma's grave, and to meet Karcsi, who waited for me sitting on a marble bench. He was my first love. I had met him at a school dance. His handsome, dark looks had captured my heart. He was tall with black hair, and he kissed well, whispering sweet little nothings in my ear. No one disturbed us during our tête-à-têtes except Szisza, the old peasant woman who cared for the graves. She looked at us from time to time, while she arranged the flowers and whispered to the dead friends she had known all her life, who lay so quiet now beneath the dark purple violets. Nothing disturbed the stillness of the cemetery, only the dramatic reds of the geraniums and the incongruity of other lovers who were kissing beside other graves.

Sometimes I would go to the cemetery alone. I would sit there for hours in the delightful lonesomeness of the damp grass, stroking the soft wild-rose petals with my fingertips. Drinking in the rapidly changing colors of the sky, I would sit there hour after hour. I felt sad, and nature helped to ease the pain of first love, and the pain of Grandma's death.

My idyllic rendezvous ended abruptly when Mother received a promotion to be the chief of Surgery in a hospital in Budapest. She broke the news to me during an evening walk after dinner, her hair glistening under the streetlights and her eyes green and secretive like moist almonds. I noticed a gaiety about her that I hadn't seen since my father's death. I was happy for her, and eager to start a new life in Budapest.

The only problem was my first love, Karcsi. He promised to write to me, but his letters never arrived at our new living quarters at Stalin Square, where we had a single room in a big apartment complex assigned to us by the Housing Bureau. We had one single room and we had to share the kitchen and the bathroom with the other tenants and with two other families who lived in the other two bedrooms. Our room had high ceilings and was filled with dark furniture, while a pale green light (like under water) came through the window that faced a blind alley. From the window I could see the Shoemakers Union, a once elegant palace that had been confiscated from its previous owners by the Union, and now had a red flag waving from the stone lion's head above the front gate.

I could also see the Liget from my window, a beautiful park with manicured flowerbeds, as well as the trollybuses, which glided along the boulevards and brightened the dullness of my days with their bright purple color.

Budapest was still a very elegant city, even with the economic disaster the Soviet regime had brought and the long lines in front of the empty stores. It was a good place to live in spite of the bribe taking, and bribe giving, and black marketeering that went on. Budapest was elegant and beautiful. The tall houses had the silkiest color, burnished by the centuries. The beautifully landscaped parks were full of flowers in season. The elaborately designed bridges connecting Pest and Buda were lit up at night, the reflection of their lights swam in the dark water of the Danube like thousands of floating stars. Because of the outstanding performances in the theaters and in the Opera House, everything was crowded night after night after night. Theater tickets were ridiculously cheap. Because food was scarce and outrageously priced, people went to see all the plays they could, and became simultaneously cultured and undernourished. As a result, there was a "who cares about tomorrow?" attitude.

To escape the bedlam of our communal kitchen, where dozens of people always waited in line in front of the stove (as well as elsewhere in front of the toilet), we often visited the Sterns who now lived in Buda in a modest apartment. We would sit on their tiny balcony looking out at the indigo mountains of Buda and talk incessantly about contemporary literature and about our new landlord, the Soviet.

The Sterns were still grieving for Tamas, who had died in a labor camp in Czechoslovakia. They had learned from a friend that he was thrown into a ditch, and that the unburied corpses would stiffen during the winter, and become soft and covered with their own yellowish juices at the first touch of spring. The stink of the rotten flesh of the Jews who were thrown into the ditch was wafted with the wind and became so overpowering that the villagers who lived close by sickened and had nightmares.

It was more comfortable to talk about Klara who now lived in Milan and was relatively happy and safe there, living in a small boarding house while waiting for a visa to Honduras. Her departure had taken place before we arrived in Budapest and been carefully planned. It happened at the

Western Railroad Terminal on a cold morning. The bare frozen branches of the trees glittered in the December sun like diamond wands, while the relatives both on the Jewish and Christian side gathered at the tracks and stood hidden behind the pillars. They held their breath while Klara boarded the train with the poised movements of a film star, dressed in a light blue winter coat with a sable collar, a dark blue hat framing her pearl-tinted oval face and enhancing the dramatic light to her bluish purple eyes. Her jet-black hair was piled high upon her head, and under it she had concealed a few valuable rings and two diamond bracelets. She could have gone to jail for smuggling jewelry out from the country. She could have been arrested on the spot if discovered. Yet she was guilty of more than that. Besides her huge green trunk filled with embroidered linen and lace underwear (from old times) she took along two bottles, one filled with wine and the other with gold coins. To fit the coins into the glass had been quite a job and taken a whole day, thoroughly exhausting Teresa who was responsible for the trick. First she filled the bottle with hot melted fat and slipped the coins down the neck of the bottle with a glass rod. The bottle was then placed overnight on the balcony in order to harden the fat in the cold air, which completed the procedure. Klara's visa had been forged, too. She got it with the aid of a recent boyfriend who had connections in the Ministry of the Interior.

With the blessing of God and with the help of Saint Antonio (a figurine of whom lay in Teresa's pocket), everything went well, and Klara was now sending interesting letters.

In the summer I graduated from the Sacred Heart convent school. After graduation, I spent a considerable amount of time in outdoor and indoor cafes to kill time and with the hope of meeting some nice young man with whom I could fall in love. One Sunday afternoon I went with Mother to a cafe on Vaci Street. While we ate our bean soup and noodles sprinkled with cheese, to the music of the newly imported blues from America and the red-headed singer sang her heart out on the low dais, I became conscious of admiring glances directed toward me by a pair of dark eyes. I returned the glances, giving clear eye signals to the young man at the next table. In a few minutes our waitress brought two schnapps sent by him with a humble request to join us. He came over and we had a delightful evening, while Mother buried herself in a magazine. His name was Peter. He was a third-year law student at the Eotvos Loranth University. I found him both handsome and amusing. Around midnight he bought me violets from the weary flowergirl, and pressed my hand under the table. The three of us walked home along the deserted dark brown night streets. He kissed our hands at our house door before he left, while I felt that I would like to take hold of his face and press my lips to his. I watched him from the door as he walked into the cloud of dust raised by the street-sweepers. Afterwards, I thought about him for a long time in the coziness of my bed. "Love has arrived!" I said to myself and welcomed its fantasies.

 Peter called the next day, and from then on we spent as much time together as possible, the city catering to us with music that floated from concert halls and beer-gardens. We sat on the steps of the Danube, our bare feet in the water, and roamed the streets where patches of sunshine always lingered in the cool ravines of the stone houses. We sat on a blanket up in the hills of Buda in a meadow and gorged ourselves on cherries and on kisses. Once we even went to a twelfth century church where we embraced among the catacombs, indifferent to the ancient skeletons that lay heaped in a dark corner.

My heart was filled with joy as I gazed at his face in the mellow light of the candles, trying to capture each moment as if it was a rare and exotic bird.

One day in 1955, we had gone to the Gellért Thermal, which dated back to the time when the Turks occupied Budapest. We soaked ourselves in the hot, sulfurous spring water in the mosaicked basins, in the water that gleamed like green silver below the golden arches of the ceiling.

We sat for a long time in the shallow water and watched the young athletes who ran past us preparing for the Olympics, and the people who drank cocktails at the white, wrought iron tables beneath the purple glare of sun lamps.

A famous young starlet was there that day from the National Theatre, flirting intently with her elderly mentor who had an Adolph-Menjou-like moustache. Then there was the curved fortyish beauty who chattered endlessly with her glossy, young gigolo, and the usual crowd of old men sitting in the hot-water baths, ogling the young girls in their minute bikinis, while steam pervaded the air. After a while we tired of all that and decided to move on to an espresso cafe where we could be alone in the privacy of a curtained alcove.

I left to get dressed, and when I returned I found Peter at a table sitting with someone I had never seen before. "This is my professor, Professor Erdes," Peter said. Then he introduced me by name.

The professor looked at me with complete indifference. He had hazel eyes and a tired yet nonetheless lively expression. In a way, he was a good-looking man, I thought, although he must be close to forty. I studied him further while he was engaged in a serious discussion with Peter about some complicated aspects of international law.

After a while he turned toward me. "You are too young to appreciate it, but the sulfurous water is good not only for the bones; it is good for the soul too. It washes away worries."

"We don't come here often," I said to him. "I prefer the Lukacs Thermal where I can swim better."

The professor looked at me now with a little more interest. There was forcefulness in his look, which contradicted his mild manners. His eyes are his most striking feature, I thought. They glow with intelligence. I noticed his hands, which were delicate and refined like a sculptor's, with sensitive fingers, and by a strange association I thought of Rodin's statue, "The Kiss."

He held out his hand to say good-bye and I put mine in his. His dry warm touch sent light tremors down my spine. All at once, he fascinated me. "I like him," I thought, "although he is a bit too old."

Riding on the trolley towards the cafe, I was confused. I couldn't explain the sudden change. The professor had been indifferent at first, and then something had happened, something unexpected. As we stood on the platform of the trolley, I leaned against Peter to protect myself from disturbing thoughts.

One month passed and the professor had completely slipped from my mind, until one day we met at Vaci Street where I had gone to do some shopping on a cold morning before Christmas. "Nice to see you," he greeted me with a genuinely warm smile. He invited me to have breakfast with him, "Some coffee and rolls and marmalade," he said, "and some good conversation."

We went into an almost empty espresso-scented cafe, where only a few people sat around the small tables. For a while we talked about the weather and drank numerous cups of coffee.

"Peter is a good student. He is a good sport too, one of the best in the class," he said later.

"He has the mind of a Greek philosopher," I said, "A very precise mind, among other good things. And he is a wonderful friend."

"Just a friend?" asked the professor with a shy smile.

I didn't answer.

"By the way," he said, "I have a few free tickets for the Music Hall for next Sunday. Debussy and Tchaikosky. Would you like to come? I will invite Peter, too; I was planning to see him."

"I am absolutely crazy about Debussy," I said, and saw his eyes light up.

"I am glad that you will come," he said.

The night before the concert Peter caught cold. He was running a high fever.

"You should go anyway," he said on the phone. "It is a good opportunity. Anyway I need good marks; talk with the professor about it," he tried to joke.

Reluctantly, I went. When I got to the Music Hall the concert had already begun. The usher guided me to my seat where the professor sat absorbed in the music, in the seawave sounds of "La Mer." As I sat down by his side, we brushed lightly against each other. I was conscious of his body against mine and a slight tremor ran through me.

"It can't be happening again!" I said to myself. "I can't believe it."

During the intermission we drank a glass of wine in the lobby. "Call me Tibor," he said after the second glass, " and let us celebrate the gifts of the gods: music, good wine, and love. Especially, love at first sight."

"In vino veritas," I said, and quite unexpectedly, I felt myself blushing.

During the second half, while the "Pathetique" hung in the air with its sweet sadness, we pretended to be deeply involved in the music.

Yet my body was conscious of the vibrations coming from his as we sat in closeness.

It feels like love, I thought— that subtle and sweet excitement. Like love. I was dominated by my instinct like an animal.

The two following months Peter was busy with his exams, and with his various meetings, where students from different universities gathered with some writers to discuss the regime. This was the first time this had happened in the history of Soviet invasion, he said. We both missed the warmth we shared in our friendship.

I sank into melancholy, and spent my days daydreaming and playing the piano, mostly my favorites "Rigoletto" and "La Traviata."

"Is there anything you want to tell me?" asked my mother.

"Have you ever been in love with two men at the same time?" I asked her.

"It can happen, I suppose," she answered.

I hoped that she was not aware that I was leading a double life under her roof, because thought I still loved Peter I thought more and more about Tibor. I wished something would happen which could lead me out of that impasse of being in love with two men, which wasn't after all such a big tragedy. I saw understanding in my mother's eyes. She was wise and she knew more than I did, knew that my confusion was the sweet confusion of youth. She knew more about me than I realized. She was my mother; I was her own flesh and blood. She knew my weaknesses and my strengths, my failures and my aspirations; she loved me the way I was in my imperfection. She was the kindest and dearest creature I ever knew and I was the world's most spoiled child.

Chapter Six
TIBOR

IT WAS A RAINY DAY when Peter next called me. It had been raining all day. It was one of those days when life seemed grey and exceptionally sad, like the rain that made the city wet and dark and weary. It wasn't the romantic kind of rain I loved, lukewarm and refreshing and smelling of the wet earth. It wasn't the melodic rain of summer either; it was cold and mean and defeating and it made me unhappy. I was glad when he called.

"I love you," he said. His voice sounded like the rain, sad and undemanding. "I am sad and frustrated and the rain doesn't help," he continued. "I couldn't marry you for another five years, you must understand! Even if everything would be all right, I must finish school and then find a job. Then we must look for a place to live. It seems hopeless, especially the question of finding an apartment. Most young people end up living with their parents in a spare room after their marriage, as you know."

"I know!" I said. "I know that you are strong and brave and that I am just the opposite. But I love you and I'll wait for you for another five years. I'll wait for you forever."

"I will call you soon," he said. "Can't wait to see you. Don't be sad about our fruitless night, don't be sad."

"I'm not sad, I'm really not," I lied.

In January I received by mail an invitation from Tibor to spend the weekend in a tourist house in the Pilis Mountains with the ski club.

"The class, Peter, and I will be there. You will enjoy the landscape and the evenings sitting round the fire, even though you are not a skier as I learn from Peter. I hope with all my heart that you will come," the letter ended.

The same afternoon, Peter called. "Are you coming, love? Please come!"

"Would you like me to come?"

"Absolutely!" he said. "I suggested to Professor Erdes that he invite you. He is an excellent skier, a brilliant conversationalist. You will enjoy his company! I want you to come. It has been such a long time. I want to hold you in my arms."

"Same here," I said.

I met them at the Western Railroad Terminal early one morning. Tibor stood surrounded by a dozen students, as if waiting anxiously just for me. He looked young and elegant in his sky blue ski jacket.

We all boarded the train. A few miles beyond Budapest the landscape was white on white, the snow whirling in eddies and lying deep in the fields and around the fences. "It will be a perfect day," said Peter, and he put his arms round me. I wondered how the day would end.

The tourist house stood on a small hill above the village with high mountains in the background. Some planks had been laid on the snow to make a path to the entrance. I stood wondering if the whole world had turned white for our pleasure: the house had whitewashed walls, the snow was bluish white, and the sky was marble white because of the snow clouds.

"It's a winter wonderland. The air smells of snow," I said.

I inhaled the fresh invigorating air of the tall pine trees and grew dizzier by the second.

"I am so happy that you are here," said Peter. "We will have a wonderful time."

I sat by the fireplace while everyone went skiing and read a book of Vicki Baum's. Then I walked in the garden and inhaled again the scent of the snow-covered garden. I was happy by myself and at sundown the group returned with windblown faces and in good spirits. We prepared dinner, everyone taking part in cooking the lentil soup and stuffed cabbage. The dinner was wonderful. We had glasses of good, cheap wine and afterwards sat around the open fire singing folk songs.

Peter kept whispering in my ear and holding my hand. He was in a romantic mood. Then I became aware of a look full of apprehension from across the big hall where Tibor sat by the window smoking his pipe.

I returned his look and forced him to meet my eyes. With a jerk he seemed to free himself from the spell we were both under. He shook off the feelings we both felt and went out to the balcony.

"I am tired," I said to Peter, and I said I must sleep. I retired to the room that the girls shared but my thoughts kept me awake. I just couldn't sleep, just couldn't sleep. Through the open door I could see Tibor's silhouette on the balcony. He stood erect in the faint light of the moon, as if waiting. I tiptoed from the room and went onto the balcony. He was not surprised to see me.

Our kiss lasted a long time.

"I have loved you the minute I saw you," he said. I leaned my head on his chest and felt the racing of his heart.

"Say it again, that you love me," I begged. He kissed me for an answer. His saliva tasted like honey, like tobacco. We stood there watching the landscape with its black woods and pale moonlight, looking mysterious and as colorless as a Japanese print.

I snuggled in his arms as trustful as a young bird. I was trembling.

"How much are you in love with Peter?" he asked me.

"I don't know. I only know I love you! You came into my life by surprise, like a comet, with the speed of a comet."

"I don't feel guilty," he said. "But we have to tell Peter."

"I don't know. I'll have to think about it. It will not be easy." Then I asked him with an anxious heart, "Have you loved before?"

"I was engaged a long time ago to a young, beautiful girl. She was like Snow White, too young and innocent, maybe like you. She didn't understand the way I loved her. She was the one who left me in the end, for another man when we were in Prague."

"You are still in love with her," I said.

"Only with the memory of her. I can't forget the sadness of the days after she left me."

"There is nothing we can do but accept our fate. "*Alea iacta est*[†]," I said.

* * *

Tibor phoned right after we got back from the mountains to ask me to go to a tea dance with him. The small ballroom was red and gold with subdued lights, and a four-man band was playing the "Tango Bolero" in the background as we entered. Waitresses glided between the small tables, dressed in black with white lace caps and aprons, like chambermaids in some operetta.

"I like it," I said. "I've never been in a place like this before. But it looks very expensive."

"It was the hand of fate that we met," he said.

We watched the young couples around us gorging themselves on tea and carrot cakes. We danced cheek to cheek to the melodies from "Ammapola." He held me tight as if he wanted to melt my body against his.

"If this is the way real love feels, I must thank God that I've discovered love," I said.

"I must find time to see you," he said. "It will not be easy. I've had a lot of meetings to go to lately. You must be patient."

"Another woman?" I asked.

"Don't be silly. I love you and you know it. And about those meetings…"

[†] The die is cast

"Don't tell me anything you don't want to," I interrupted. "It is your business. I am happy just to be with you."

"Tomorrow I will be free. We could go to Margaret Island, to the Grand Hotel. There is a French chef there who can still make bouillabaisse from our lake fish."

"I've never eaten bouillabaisse, never been to the Grand Hotel. It would be wonderful."

"I want to show you Budapest. I want to dine you and wine you and to buy you flowers. I will ask the *cigany primas*† to play your favorite song on the violin, just for you."

"Then I'll cry my eyes out," I answered.

I waited for his call in vain. I was hurt when a week had passed, angry by the second week, desperate by the third.

At the end of the third week the phone rang. It was a woman's voice on the other end. "It's about Tibor," she said. "He was picked up at his house a few weeks ago by the secret police. One more thing… He is in the political jail on Main Street."

I couldn't believe it. I couldn't understand what had happened. I cried for weeks after the unknown woman's call and I roamed the colorless winter streets with tears flowing from my eyes.

Spring arrived with harsh colors and scents. Then all the spring flowers died, and summer was here with new fragrances and new songs, and a constant hot wind blowing across the Danube turned its water to dirty green. The cafes were filled with people earnestly flirting. The city was bathed in starlight and music, and I was alone. I had never seen so many lovers as I saw that summer, kissing on benches and in doorways. I watched them with an aching heart as

† Gypsies

they passed through the glass doors of the restaurants. The amorous singing of the popular Russian tunes that blared from the loudspeakers in every square heightened my loneliness. Every cell of my body yearned for love, more strongly than ever now that I had none. I spent the summer waiting for letters from Peter who was in a distant village with his classmates, by order of the government, to help the farmers with the harvest. Other than that I had nothing to do to keep my boredom at bay.

I read books to lift my spirit but they were the wrong books, Werther and Flaubert. They undermined my usually healthy feelings.

By fall a strange melancholy pervaded my days, wrapping me in a silken net, like the perfume of decadence.

Strangely enough, I emerged from all this refreshed like a flower after rain. I looked in the mirror and saw my own face, pale yet interesting.

"You look like an adolescent boy, thin and wispy," said Mother.

"You look younger than your age. It will be an advantage when you pass thirty," said Gaby. She was a sophisticated lady who lived close to us and was married to a Jewish newspaper writer. He was twenty years her senior, a red-haired man with an aquiline nose, and an opinionated air about him. They would walk hand in hand exchanging loving smiles.

I was invited to a garden party at their home one day in September. The party was held behind their house in a small garden whose fading fall flowers gave off their strong scents without a trace of guilt, like older women in love. For a while I mingled with the guests, avant-garde writers of the regime with their mistresses, and writers from former times with their wives. Meanwhile, Gaby glided over the pebblestones offering demitasse and rum and watching her husband with jealous, dark, gleaming eyes. (He was trying out one of his unpublished novels on the guests, reading it aloud and watching the girls' reaction, a complicated undertaking). I noticed that Gaby watched him with devotion, while he eyed my thighs and appraised my breasts. I was obviously the youngest of the guests and it made me slightly embarrassed.

It was after midnight when he approached me and proposed a rendezvous at the Hotel Astoria the following day, or at any other hotel where we could have a midday meal. I accepted his invitation out of sheer boredom.

We met somewhere in Buda and sat in the fall garden at a table for two, the sun shining on our faces. I satisfied myself on the pink Italian ice and a slice of Dobos Torte, while he tried to talk me into going upstairs and spending the rest of the day in a room. "No one would ever guess where we had been," he said. "You needn't worry."

I finished the ice and excused myself, saying I must go to the ladies' room, and I left by a back door.

It is useless, useless, useless, I thought. I can't supplant Tibor, not even with an interesting writer. I am not Lucrezia Borgia. I am a lonely seeker after love, in vain.

Chapter Seven
REVOLUTION

IN THE FIRST WEEK of October, Peter phoned. I was glad to hear his voice as I hadn't heard from him for a long time.

"There's going to be a demonstration on October 23rd. I want you to come," he said. "I'm dying to see you, but I can't before the demonstration, I'm afraid. We're organizing it to express our deep sympathy with the solidarity of the Polish youth in connection with events in Poland. We're asking for all Russian troops to leave Hungary. We've reached the point when we dare to say that publicly."

"I didn't know, it's a surprise to me that you are so involved in politics," I said.

"It'll be at the statue of Bern," he said. "Will you come?"

"I'll think it over," I said, "You know very well how little interest I take in politics…"

"Please try to come, my love, come for my sake."

Early afternoon as I left the house on October 23rd the streets were already packed with people. I had never seen so many on the streets at that hour, as if all work in Budapest had come to a standstill.

It was a beautiful fall day, gold and red autumn leaves drifting, a hot wind blowing from the direction of the blue mountains of Buda. And something holiday-like in the air. I couldn't understand it.

Maybe it was the "sixteen points" the students had posted everywhere on walls and on buildings. People grew emotional when they read them.

"There's not a typist or stenographer in Budapest who doesn't spend most of the day copying down the points," said an old lady who wore a flame-colored poncho and had a happy smile on her withered lips. "Against the wishes of the Communist Party, hundreds are marching on the streets; and in spite of the orders of the Ministry of Interior, who has forbidden any public meetings or demonstrations until further notice."

A young secretary said she had heard the Writers Club broadcasting to Europe in French from Radio Budapest, suggesting the need for the Party to disclose in all honesty the economic situation in the country.

"I couldn't believe that I was hearing that on the radio," she said.

"The Polish Party Central Committee elected National Communist Wladislaw Gomulka at the October 19-20 meeting, and defied the threats of Soviet force being used," a young boy declared enthusiastically, seemingly deeply moved.

The city was beginning to look like an anthill, as the crowds grew. A young robust peasant woman was busy pinning cockades in the Hungarian colors on the lapels of people's coats— colors that were not allowed to be worn during the Russian occupation. She pinned one on my lapel too.

Hundreds of university students advanced, waving their flags, students of technology, law, medicine, economics and all, along with students from other universities, led by their professors. I searched in vain for Peter among them.

I started to move with the crowd. Young workers came from nearby factories and joined the students. Soon, passersby and motorists joined, swelling the numbers. I heard that the People's Army had joined the crowd, approximately eight hundred of them as people estimated. Students were handing out Hungarian and Polish flags, shouting, "Long live the young of Poland." A feverish excitement painted faces red, lit up eyes. By the time we got to the statue of Bern, the crowd must have numbered 50,000. We sang the National Anthem. A speaker arose and addressed the crowd. His voice was carried by the warm autumn wind.

"We have come to a historical point," he said. "We demand independent national policy based on the principle of socialism. Workers should run factories. The peasants should be assured the right of free self-determination. We believe that we are expressing the wishes of the whole nation."

At the end of the speech we all streamed across the Danube to the Parliament Building and we shouted in unison demanding that the light on a large red star on the top of the building be extinguished. As the light went out, there were cheers, screams, and cries. People just stood there in the growing darkness. It was all very emotional and I could feel a choking sensation in my throat.

It took me a good two hours to walk home on the crowded streets where people still gathered under the streetlights engaged in feverish conversation, and where even the houses seemed different from yesterday, looking somehow more solid and real and in much brighter colors than ever before. I was on the verge of exhaustion. All I wished for was to go to bed and contemplate the events of the day. I longed for a cup of strong tea and hoped to find some bread and sugar on the kitchen shelves. As I rounded the corner of Stalin Square where my house stood I saw a mob of people at the Square, a mob that burst and swelled like the sea, I knew right away that something extraordinary was happening. As I looked more I noticed people working like crazy on the huge statue of Stalin with hammers and steel bars. Then I saw Stalin falling from his pedestal, most ungracefully. It was a shocking and glorious moment, judging from the cheers and screams and cries, and although I was too tired to scream, a strong excitement invaded my body like good old wine. People still screamed and others joined the celebration, watching from the windows of the surrounding houses. Before I entered the front door of my house, I cast one more look at the torso of Stalin lying in the dust and saw some street urchins climb to the top of the big boots of Stalin, which remained on the pedestal and urinate happily into their depth.

I was lucky. My mother had apparently been home, because I found a half loaf of bread and a lemon on the shelves, and a note assuring me of her love. I put on the kettle, sliced the bread and the lemon, and with the anticipation of a peaceful evening started to call Peter's house. I called all night, in vain. No one was home.

I went out at dawn hoping to find him somewhere. There were few people on the streets, mostly men in pairs, who disappeared into hallways. Along Stalin Square and throughout the town, cafes and stores were all closed.

Cinemas and theaters were shut. As I passed the district where the Soviet officers and their families lived, the elegant villas looked abandoned and the gardens with their wrought-iron fences lay strangely silent as if the tenants had left in a hurry. I didn't get farther than Terez Ring where I found all the roads and streets leading to the Radio Station closed. A National Guard stopped me and advised me to go home. I turned back and found an open Pub. I went in and asked for a bowl of pea soup. I thought that the girl sitting on my side of the long table looked familiar. Then I remembered seeing her in the past walking around the Opera House, her inviting crimson lips trying to lure clients into her small house.

"Business is lousy nowadays," she turned to me. "Men are busy building barricades."

"I know," I said. "I know."

After lunch, I found an open bakery and bought a loaf of stale bread. Then I decided to go to Magda's house. Peter and I used to go to her house to learn English from her, reciting solemnly "Baa Baa black sheep, have you any wool?" I asked her if she had heard anything from Peter.

"I have not seen him for ages." she told me. She looked like an aging angel by Murillo, relaxed and fat, refined and cultured right down to her fortyish baroque bottom. Before I left, I gave her half my bread. She gave me in exchange a small package of cocoa.

"I've got more," she said. "It is from an American Care Package. I was going to save it for Christmas. But who knows, we might not be around."

I went home, walking on the carpet of falling leaves, and pretending that the boulevards were the Via Veneto, the Latin Quarter, and the Kurfurstendamm where I had never been. It was my favorite game. I pretend that nothing was wrong although the houses looked like gray prison walls, the lightless windows like blind eyes, and the bridges over the Danube as fragile as a cobweb in the dusk.

Peter came in round midnight, pale, exhausted and listless, as if he was drained of all emotion. "My father is dead," he said. His eyes were like a lake after a storm, strangely colorless, his face haggard.

I learned that following the demonstration he had gone with the students to the radio station, demanding that the sixteen points be broadcast. The narrow streets around the station had been closely packed when they got there, soldiers and workers spilling over into the adjacent streets.

"None of us were armed," he said.

A few students had gone to the radio station to try to negotiate terms. All their terms had been denied, and the delegation had been arrested. Rumors spread that one student had been shot inside. At the news the uproar from the crowd grew thunderous. Reinforcement of the secret police arrived, carrying rifles and bayonets. From one of the nearby houses hoses were turned on the crowd. Then some of the crowd began to force their way into the radio building.

By then the streets had grown very dark and chilly. Suddenly, tear gas began to be sprayed from the upper floor of the radio building. AVH men rushed out, shooting in all directions, wounding and killing several people in the crowd. Friends and fellow workers carried off the dead, while others followed in procession. Ambulances arrived with men in white uniforms, who turned out to be secret police in disguise. They poured out of the ambulances, their weapons hidden under their white doctors' coats. It was then that all hell broke loose.

"We attacked them," said Peter. "Workers and the students alike, sons of Communists, like myself."

Trucks with Hungarian officers had arrived, the "Peoples Army,"— declaring that they would not shoot their own flesh and blood. Then fire opened up again from the radio building, killing several of the officers of the People's Army. Shortly after that Peter had seen his father ride up on a truck filled with steelworkers. They had rushed over, carrying weapons they had picked up on their way from the military barracks and from the police. "We fought side by side with Father until he was killed by a single bullet. He died instantly."

"You are shivering," I said, "I'll prepare a hot bath. I'll fix hot cocoa while you are soaking in the tub…" I left him in the bathroom and went out to the kitchen to put the water on. I cut a thick slice of bread and put everything neatly on a tray. Then I suddenly heard strange noises going on outside. They sounded like tanks approaching. I ran to the window. Outside in the semi-darkness, I saw sure enough that two Soviet tanks were parked right across the street and faced the house. Then the thunder of the cannon seemed to split my eardrums. The house began to shake. I fell on my knees, but got up quickly and made my way through the rubble and dust toward the bathroom.

Peter was sitting in the tub with a peaceful expression on his face, as if sleeping. Blood oozed from his temple from a wound and dyed the water red.

For a long time I stood there frozen in horror.

"There was so much I wanted to tell you, my love," I said to him at last. "But it is too late." I closed his eyes and stayed with him. I wanted to scream my heart out. But I stayed with him crying, while the death-dealing work continued outside on the streets.

No one can console a man for having to die.

Mother found me in a state of shock when she arrived home from the hospital the next day. All too familiar with death, she calmly took action. "We must bury him outside the park," she said. "The roads are closed, including the one leading to the central cemetery. It took me hours to walk home. I came on back roads. There are street fights everywhere."

Rain started to fall as we carried Peter outside, covered with a red curtain I had taken down from the window. We took turns digging the earth, and we both wept.

"We are losing all touch with the realities of life, but we must carry on!" Mother said.

I thought that God was punishing me for having been in love with two men.

We crept back to the house later to try to salvage some things from the debris in our room. People were wandering among the ruined apartments, some old women crying hysterically. But within a few days, everyone had calmed down and begun to set up households together, sharing a slice of bread, a cigarette, and a little food. Solidarity flourished as never before. I wondered if disaster might not have its merit in bringing out the best in people.

Peter's lonely grave was soon surrounded with others. There were temporary graves in the park. Some of the dead freedom fighters were buried on the spot where they fell, with only a bloodstained, bullet-ridden jacket, a single shoe, or a pair of eyeglassses on the graves for identification.

October 25, 1956

Soviet tanks surrounded Budapest, and there was savage fighting in the streets. I was confined to my room but Mother went back to the hospital. I was alone. I heard on the radio that the Party Central Committee was promising to begin negotiations for the withdrawal of Soviet troops. The radio was the only source of information. I was glued to it all day long. There wasn't much food in the house, and I didn't sleep well. I felt constantly afraid.

October 26, 1956

I heard on the radio that the freedom fighters were in control of Western Hungary and the entire frontier bordering Austria. I listened all the time to Radio Free Europe and the Voice of America. I listened to five other free broadcasting stations, which were operated by the freedom fighters. That day I went out, as it was relatively quiet. I bought the first free newspaper which I found people feverishly reading on the streets.

October 27, 1956

Carloads of food arrived from Poland. The freedom fighters were in control of the political situation. I was able to go to the market with Miriam. She was a widow, a nice Jewish woman who lived on the third floor with her three boys, who were always hungry. We arrived home richer by two kilos of flour, a bag of sugar, which was distributed by the freedom fighters to everyone, and a fat goose. Later we killed and plucked and roasted the goose and we ate it down to the bones.

Mother arrived home in time for the feast. She was busy now in the hospital taking care of hundreds of wounded. She told us that the International Red Cross had sent them a large supply of bandages and blood plasma from the United States.

October 28, 1956

The Hungarian security police had virtually ceased to exist. They were discarding their uniforms, and were in hiding.

We knew all that because someone always brought us news from the streets. Today I heard that two Italian newspapermen had arrived in Budapest who said that the inhabitants here fought very gallantly the past four days. They also observed that on some occasions Soviet tanks sided with the insurgents. The two Italian journalists were asked to identify themselves at the city limits by the Soviets; when they said that they were Italian journalists, the soldiers cheered for Garibaldi and wished them luck.

The oil workers continued to strike until the Soviets left Hungary. Thirty wagonloads of coal were waiting to be sent immediately to factories and to the population, the radio said. I wished I could get hold of some coal because my room was cold. I was burning old newspapers in the tiled stove, but that didn't give much heat. The radio also said that we would get coal only on condition that the Soviets left our country.

October 29, 1956

Imre Nagy† ordered a ceasefire. Much of the fighting on the streets stopped, largely on the freedom fighters' terms. Negotiations on the withdrawal of Soviet troops had begun, said the radio. I also heard that the Hungarian air force had threatened to blow up Soviet tanks if they remained in Budapest. News was still coming in from the streets, good and bad.

Last night I dreamed that I was with both Peter and Tibor in a room with dimmed lights. They both asked me to dance and I couldn't decide which one to accept.

Today mother came home. She arrived, bringing milk, two eggs, a little sugar, and a half-loaf of bread. We had a nice breakfast. After breakfast she went back to the hospital. She looked fatigued. "I hate to leave you by yourself," she said. "You must take care."

I was happy to have a visitor in the afternoon. Magda came in with a young boy whom she introduced as her nephew. He was a nice boy with bright blue eyes and a good face. But he was pale now and looked ill.

"I picked him up close to the house," said Magda. "He was trembling. We must cover him with a blanket." It turned out that the boy had been among the crowd of people who were heading that morning toward the Parliament from the hotel Astoria to make a peaceful demonstration expressing the wish of the Nation that the Soviet troops leave Hungary. They had gathered in front of the hotel when three Soviet tanks drove up beside the Western Railroad Station and opened fire on them.

"We dispersed into the side streets," said the boy, talking feverishly as if talking would relieve his tension.

† the new premier minister

"A little later I went back to the hotel and saw eight Soviet tanks standing there, the crew in friendly conversation with the people who inquired why the other Soviet tanks had fired on us before. During the discussion, the Soviet captain, a tall young man with a kind face, said that he felt our demonstration was justified. We were thrilled when he ordered his men to accompany us to the Parliament. I sat with him in the first tank to lead the way. Upon our arrival, there were an estimated 25,000 or more people in the Square waiting for the Prime Minister, Imre Nagy, to appear. Many were women and children. Soon after our arrival with the friendly Soviet tanks, someone from the rooftop of the building opened fire on the crowd with a machine gun. Suddenly, other Soviet tanks approached from the side streets and fire was exchanged between the Soviet on our side and the ones against us. There were screams and moans, people collapsed— men, women, children. There was panic. It was impossible to estimate the number of the dead. An ambulance arrived, carrying a woman doctor and two nurses; they were shot before they could help." Thoroughly exhausted, in the middle of his story, the boy fell asleep.

We went to the window where we could see a huge crowd coming, carrying bloodsoaked Hungarian flags and clothing that had belonged to the people shot down in the front of the Parliament. Thousands were marching. An old, gray-haired peasant woman, a soldier, and a priest were leading the march. Later we learned that about 800 people had been killed at the Parliament and about twelve truckloads of corpses were removed from the Square.

"There is rumor that the doors of political jails will be opened tomorrow morning by the freedom fighters," said Magda.

My heart skipped a beat. "I might see Tibor tomorrow," I thought. I asked Magda to stay for the night so that we could walk to the jail together the next morning.

To pass the time, she began to tell me a story dating back to 1945 when she was thirty years old. "The Soviet troops had just taken Budapest from the Germans after two months of siege," she said. "Raping and atrocities were going on all over town. I had a nice-looking Soviet captain billeted in my house. He came from those unending steppes of the Caucasus. He was blond and blue-eyed and I was lucky that he was also gentle and kind. I gave him my bedroom and slept in the parlor myself. I still remember the balalajka music that drifted through the open window. It was a hot and windless night and I couldn't sleep. Then I suddenly saw him approaching my bed— stark naked— his Slavic eyes mysterious in the moonlight. From then on, he came every night for about three weeks. I fell in love with him."

"I am happy for you," I said. "You have beautiful memories."

We arrived at the jail just in time and saw the prisoners coming out in small groups. They looked haggard and gave off a stale smell as they walked slowly through the gates.

I stood there, my heart racing, hoping that Tibor would be among them. I was just about to give up hope when he suddenly appeared before my eyes like an apparition, pale and unshaved.

He caught sight of me and his face took on a look of such joy and sadness that it was almost impossible to bear. He took me in his arms. "Freedom feels almost sensuous; it is like being in love," he said.

We both cried.

The sun came out from behind thick clouds; in the sudden light, he appeared taller and years younger than I had remembered him.

Chapter Eight
SHATTERED DREAMS

HE WALKED TOWARD HIS HOUSE past broken-down streetcars and abandoned barricades. The city lay quietly like a strong woman after giving birth, listless from loss of blood.

On the winding streets of Buda the pastel-tinted villas were asleep like butterflies in the early darkness, of a fall afternoon. His house stood in desolation, the garden by the front gate overgrown and neglected. The house looked haunted when we got there, a few magnificent old trees lining the path. We jumped over tall, tangled weeds, and for a while sat on the worn stone steps and fallen pine needles. Then we went inside. The rooms were sparsely furnished and they looked as sorrowful as the house, a silky, powdery dust covering it all. Only the mellow colors of some velvety oriental rugs brightened the scene and relieved the sadness of the peeling walls.

He left the room and returned with a basket of logs, I helped to stoke the tiled stove, which stood in the corner white and beautiful like a pregnant bride. Later we sat in front of it while the fire crackled and filled the room with warmth. He turned on the radio and we heard a nasal voice announce: "The Party and the Government are making every effort to restore order… Factories are opening, the workers are returning to their job. Streetcar rails are being repaired for restoration of service in certain lines…"

"You must be hungry," he said. "I don't have anything except some bread I brought with me from jail. There must be some duck fat left on the shelf in a jar…"

"Splendid," I said. Bread spread with duck fat used to be my favorite meal, in the sunny days of my childhood…"

He found a half bottle of wine somewhere and poured it into crystal, goblets. "Let's drink to our love," he said. "It's too bad that the wine seems to have lost its strength while I was in jail. Its color remained the same though, yellow gold, just like your hair."

"I have sad news for you," I said. "…about Peter. He is dead…"

Tibor looked at me with horror. He poured more wine for us. "Tell me everything!" he asked me.

He listened quietly while I told him. He somehow maintained his calm while I sobbed between each sentence. When I ended my story and told him how we buried Peter in the park, his face already pale from his time in jail turned whiter. "Oh God, Oh Merciful God", he said, "And we don't even have the luxury of mourning him in the proper way."

"Don't look at me like that," I cried. "I feel as though I am betraying Peter's memory by loving you more than I loved him."

Tibor took me in his arms and gently shook me. "Cry, cry my Love," he said. "The tears will wash out the sadness of your heart. I am with you. We will cherish Peter's memory together." He walked me to the window, opening its shutters wide to allow the cold air to cool my burning face.

Later on we sat at the front of the fire, I asked him to tell me about his arrest. He told me that in 1951 he had joined an underground group who opposed the totolitarian and atheistic ideology of the Soviet just as much as they had opposed the Nazis.

"But what were you actually doing? Why did they arrest you really? Were you conspiring to overthrow the Communist government?" I asked him.

"We were more realistic than to try that. All we were doing was to prepare for free elections by working out a detailed platform on democratic principles and the Judeo-Christian ideology, in contrast to the Marxist one. But even to consider free elections was a major crime in the eyes of the regime, as my AVH interrogators told me in jail."

"I might never have seen you again were it not for the revolution," I said.

"A revolution in which Peter and many young people died so I could become free." His eyes were moist with tears. "I only hope they didn't die in vain… I hope there is a new life ahead for the nation. We will build a new society where individual freedom and social justice will go hand in hand."

"You still haven't told me the details of your arrest," I interrupted him. "Your friend Vera said she didn't even know what you were doing."

Tibor told me that they were careful to screen every person before they allowed him or her to join their group. They especially didn't want anyone who already had problems with the police, knowing that the people who were under police surveillance could lead to the discovery of the group.

> We were successful for five years. Then one of our group, a nice tall guy who always seemed in good spirits, was arrested for selling nylon stockings on the black market. He did it to support his wife and five children. After a while he was released from jail but the secret police forced him to reveal our identities and activities, threatening him with a return to jail if he refused.
>
> With every available cruelty they forced him to tell them the names of the group leaders, eleven men and two women, including me. Although we lived in different sections of the city, we were arrested on the same night so we could not warn each other.

He told me that each of them was aware his or her life was in danger, that the Communist government could only be overthrown by force before free elections could be held. That force could only be armed revolution or a war, which the USA would win. I felt admiration for his group and him being so brave and I wanted to hear more. He told me that they came to his apartment about midnight, the night after we had been to the tea dance…

"They burst into my room, four tough-looking men dressed in civilian clothes, political investigators from the secret police. They searched my room, ripping open the mattresses, ransacking everything."

"They wanted to catch you and tortue you because your ideal was absolute freedom for the individual like in the United States." I told him. "It is a horrible thing to do!"

They did torture me... later on. First they continued to search every book in my library until they found what they wanted— the only copy of our political program and a draft of a new Constitution. After about two hours of searching and using abusive language they dragged me outside where their car was waiting. They pushed me into the car. A half hour later I found myself in the basement of the jail where they put me in one of the locker alongside the wall. I had to stand there in the dark for a long time. Later when I was completely exhausted they took me to another room where I had to strip naked. After kicking me a few times, a sergeant took away all my belongings and gave me a prison uniform. From then on, I was 'prepared' for the trial. I was taken to an evil-smelling room every day, a smoke-filled room where the interrogating major and a five-man squad of guards were waiting. I knew I could expect no mercy, when I saw their distorted, hatred-filled, sadistic faces. They used obscene language. They wanted me to sign papers with lies about crimes that I never committed. When I refused, the beating began again. We were kicked and beaten, deprived of sleep, and forced (some of us) to take narcotics and mind-impairing drugs. I met prisoners with burned fingernails, and men who had lost their manhood as a result of mutilation.

"I can't stand it. Please, my Love." I said. "Forgive my weakness. Tell me everything and let me share it with you."

"They wanted to break us down mentally and physically," he continued. "They wanted us to confess to 'crimes' committed against the Peoples' Republic. They produced 'Show Trials' where most of the representatives of the European press would be present. At nights I could hear the cries and groans coming from the torture chambers."

"I am so happy that you are here with me," I sobbed.

The room became chilly. I went to the window to close it and was taken aback to see down below, that the city was glowing with thousands of flickering candles, as far as my eyes could see. Then I remembered that it was the night of All Saints' Day.

"Budapest is lighting every window in memory of the dead freedom fighters!" I cried. I found a candle and placed it on the windowsill to join the other mourners. The two of us stood by the window for a long time, Tibor's arms around me while his lips rested lightly on my temple. I had no desire to move.

We slept a few hours on the Persian rug in front of the tiled stove. Early in the morning we rode down from the Hill of Roses on a rusty bicycle he found in the toolhouse.

"I must go to a meeting of my underground group," he said.

"We have to discuss what actions we should take now that we may have a chance of realizing our plans to build a free and just society."

We reached the Margit Boulevard, one of the main thoroughfares of Buda, and Tibor stopped every now and again to read the posters on the walls. Some denounced Rakosi, the deposed dictator, others announced newly formed revolutionary and workers' councils, demanded economic reforms, freedom of speech and political action, called for new elections with all parties participating.

He seized a newspaper from the first newsstand and hungrily devoured the pages. "It is like a dream!" he said. "Just two days ago I resigned to spending ten to fifteen years in prison and now this feeling of freedom! Reforms we were planning in secret are now being demanded openly by broad segments of the population. If we have free elections as requested in these posters, we have an excellent chance of becoming the majority party if we succeed in uniting all the groups of similar persuasion!"

Suddenly, we came on a large group of people gathered round a Hungarian army truck that had stopped in the middle of the street. A young captain was standing on the truck to read aloud a proclamation of the Revolutionary Council of the Air Force, which demanded the complete withdrawal of the Soviet Army. Tibor became even more excited, his face flushed. "Let's go!" he urged me. "I can hardly wait to start actively participating instead of just listening. Events move fast in times like this."

At Marx Square we had to part; I had to go home, he to the meeting. "Call me as soon as you are free," I begged him, and I kissed him passionately as if it was for the last time.

"Of course I will," he answered a little impatiently. I could see that his thoughts were already at the meeting. The excitement on his face made him look very handsome and I loved him more than ever. I clung to him, but even so, it was a hasty embrace, lasting only as long as it took him to get on his bicycle.

It was late in the evening when the phone finally rang. It was Tibor. "I miss you!" he said. "But we had an interesting meeting with representatives of several Christian Democratic groups, among them my favorite party, the Democratic People's Party. It was the largest opposition party in 1947. We got a message from Cardinal Mindszenty warning us not to split up the non-marxist forces into too many parties."

"Tell me more," I begged him. "I want to hear everything!"

He continued to tell me that a small delegation including him was sent to the Parliament building to meet Premier Imre Nagy, in order to notify him officially about the formation of the Christian Front as a political party for which they had worked out a detailed platform during the past five years. When they arrived they were told to wait because Premier Nagy had a meeting with Soviet Ambassador Yuri Andropov. After about ten minutes, a door opened and Andropov came out.

"He looked grave and in a hurry as he passed us," said Tibor. "He looked at us with cold blue eyes, nodded without a smile and left."

An aid of Imre Nagy then told them the big news. The reason the Premier had invited Yuri Andropov to his office was to notify him that Hungary had decided to withdraw from the Warsaw Pact and was declaring neutrality, asking the Soviet, the U.S.A., Hngland and France to guarantee that neutrality, in the way they had done with Austria.

"I am overwhelmed!" I said. "It is too good to be true! Does that mean that the Soviet troops will move out?"

"I don't trust the Soviet Ambassador," he said. "I don't trust Yuri Andropov. There was something about him that gave me the creeps. I cannot believe that they will let us go free so easily, but let's hope for the best. Tomorrow we meet with the leaders of the Revolutionary Youth Party who want to join our Christian Front, so I won't be able to see you, my love. Saturday, meetings again, but Sunday will be all ours. This will be my first Sunday out of prison. We will celebrate."

"I am in love with you. I put a lock on my hands and my desire. I want you for my whole life, not just for now. I want to put a wedding ring on your finger and have you with me forever."

"You are all I want in the world," I said and was struck cold with fear that I would not see him anymore.

"I will call soon," he said.

"I will wait for your call day and night."

* * *

I thought about him all the time, after he had disappeared on his bicycle into the honey-colored Budapest afternoon. That was three days ago. He never called. I was worried. I heard on the radio that Hungary had now been invaded by Soviet troops from Romania and Czekoslovakia. A freedom fighter told us that the Russians occupied all the strategic points in Eastern Hungary— bridges, railway lines, and crossings. Someone had seen Soviet tanks surrounding the Uranium mines at Pecs.

November 4, 1956

Today at dawn I woke up to some strange sounds coming from the street below. It was unmistakably the thunder of cannons. I woke up drenched with perspiration from a nightmare and believed that the continuous blasts were part of my dreams. I went to the window. The streets were completely deserted except for Soviet tanks with huge red stars painted on their sides. I turned on the radio and heard our Premier, Imre Nagy, addressing the nation:

> This is Imre Nagy speaking. Today at daybreak, Soviet troops attacked our capital with the obvious intent of overthrowing the legal democratic Hungarian government. Our troops are in combat. The government is at its post. I am notifying the people of our country and the entire world of this fact.

The announcement was repeated in English, Russian, French, and Hungarian for the next couple of hours. There was a report at 6:45 from New York. The Associated Press announced that the United States had asked the Security Council of the United Nations, early that morning, to hold an emergency meeting on Sunday to discuss the Soviet offensive in Hungary. The report was submitted by American Ambassador Henry Cabot Lodge less than an hour after news agencies gave notice of large-scale Soviet attacks all over Hungary. Lodge requested the Council Chairman to hold the meeting earlier should the situation deteriorate.

At 10 a.m., I heard the manifesto of the Hungarian Writers:

> Attention, Attention, to every writer in the World, to all scientists, to all writers' federations, to all science academies and associations, to all the intelligentsia of the world. We ask all of you for support and help. There is very little time! You know the facts; there is no need to give you a special report! Help Hungary! Help the Hungarian writers, scientists, workers, peasants, and our intelligentsia! Help! Help! Help! S.O.S! S.O.S! S.O.S!

I was completely alone in the house. Mother was at the hospital and the communist tenants had disappeared from the house. They were probably hiding. At noon I heard Dunapentele calling Europe in Hungarian, Italian, French and German:

> Attention! Attention! This morning at dawn, Russian forces launched a general attack on the Hungarian Nation. We ask the United Nations to send immediate help! We ask for parachute troops to be dropped over Western Hungary. It is possible that our broadcast will soon stop and you will hear us no more. We will only be silent when we are massacred!

After repeating this several times, their broadcast was interrupted and they were never heard from again.

I didn't feel like eating at all during the day, just sat listening to the radio. I left the radio on all night long.

November 5, 1956

This morning at dawn, I heard an unidentified station, location unknown, announcing:

> Civilized people of the world, listen and come to our aid, not with declarations but with force, with soldiers and with arms. There is no stopping the wild onslaught of Bolshevism. Your turn will also come, once we perish. Save our souls! Our ship is sinking! Light is failing the shadows grow darker and darker every hour over the soil of Hungary… Extend your fraternal hand. S.O.S., S.O.S., God be with you.

At 7:25 a.m. Radio Free Kossuth went off the air with repeated S.O.S signals. The station was silent until 8 a.m. When transmission resumed, it was in the hands of a Soviet-controlled regime.

Around noon, Miriam arrived, pale and frightened. "I didn't sleep all night long," she said. "I'm scared. There are savage battles going on on the streets… The Soviet leaders must see that they cannot change the beliefs of our nation by using cannons and bayonets."

November 6, 1956

Savage fighting on the streets. Freedom fighters blew up jet fighters on a Soviet airfield in Papa. There is heavy fighting in various districts, in the suburbs. This morning our house was hit again, this time by small Soviet bombers. Outside the air was filled with smoke from burning buildings as I ran down to the cellar with the other tenants from every floor… making our way through dust and broken glass and debris… people stumbling and children crying. The cellar was dark and wet and filled with people and the raw smell of spiders crushed underfoot. Someone's portable radio played Beethoven's Funeral March. People's faces expressed despair, fear, and anguish. Right after the music, the speaker announced that the Soviet troops were closing in on Budapest. I sat in a corner with Miriam and her three sons as she handed out small pieces of graying chocolate to everyone around. "I saved it from someone's birthday cake," she said. The piece of old graying chocolate melted on my tongue and oddly reminded me of the Gerbauds, Budapest's most fashionable confectionary. Mother and I used to frequent it in better days to buy their well-known sweets. I must be crazy, thinking of the vanilla-scented, crystal-and-baroque cafes of prewar Hungary while bombs are falling outside and the revolution won a few short days ago at such a great price is dying.

When we finally came up from the cellar, we saw that some of the floors were badly damaged. Several families had lost their homes. A freedom fighter came in from the street asking for some food and water and told us that some 200,000 fresh troops had been brought in from Mongolia to take over the strategic points of Budapest and to suppress the resistance. "These troops sent in by Kruschev don't even know they are in Budapest," he said. "They thought they were being sent to the Middle East to fight the Israelis, the French and the British. Looking at the Danube the Russian soldiers kept asking, "Is that the Suez Canal?"

* * *

    Today word spread through the house about an organized women's demonstration against the Soviet tanks that were stationed in front of the Parliament. I went to the Square where the demonstration was said to be held and joined the thousands of women waiting there, dressed in dark clothes and holding aloft forests of red white and green national flags, from which the Communist coat of arms had been cut out. The women stood face to face with the mongolian soldiers who manned the tanks.

    We stood in stillness in the defused light, which seeped through the amethest-colored clouds in the sky. Then suddenly a church bell chimed the hour and as if at a signal someone called, *"Russkiy*†, go home!"

    It started as a whisper, and rose like thunder, our voices echoing against the stone walls of the Square. "Russkiy go home! Russkiy go home!"

    We moved toward the tanks. I was in front with a young girl on my right, who had tired and old-looking eyes. A white-haired peasant woman marched on my left whose innocent, blue-eyed stare was young and relaxed.

---

†   a Russian person

I moved toward the tanks with anger such as I'd never known before. I felt such unspeakable hatred against the Soviets and everything they stood for that it seemed as if my heart would burst from hatred. That feeling gave me an almost superhuman strength and I almost believed I could break the steel ring of nearing tank treads with my bare hands. The tanks advanced. At that moment my political consciousness was born. Suddenly, I didn't care about my own life, I was ready to sacrifice it for the sake of justice, and I fully understood the political beliefs of Peter and Tibor.

One of the Mongolian soldiers reached out from one tank and grabbed the young girl who was marching on my right, holding her in midair as though she were a fish on a hook. I tried to pull her back. The Soviet soldier cursed me! The old woman on my left pulled at the hem of the girl's skirt in vain. The young girl was dragged inside the tank. Shots were fired. Screaming, the women ran after the tank. More shots were fired and we dispersed in all directions…

When I turned around I saw tanks circling in the Square, shooting in the air— noise, screaming, confusion.

The memory of the girl who disappeared inside the Soviet tank still haunts my nights, I heard that even the children of twelve to fourteen who fought against the Soviets were now being accused of participating in the revolt and kept in prison until they reach sixteen, the lowest age at which capital punishment is legal. Their crime was to have resisted, with only their bare hands and Molotov cocktails, the 2,000 tanks and 70,000 Soviet troops armed with all the artillery and aircraft then stationed in Budapest.

November 8, 1956

Now began the mass deportation of freedom fighters to the U.S.S.R. Countries such as India, Burma, Ceylon, Indonesia were asking for the withdrawal of all Soviet troops from Hungary. Widespread strikes were paralyzing industry in Budapest; the shelves of the stores were bare. There is almost nothing to eat in the house, but I was not even hungry. I listen all day to the radio, my only source of information. I listen to the radio day and night. At night when the city lies in morbid silence, I remember foreign journalists used to refer to our joie de vivre and our will to live and call Budapest "little Paris"— referring to my city when it used to glitter at night before the Soviet invasion. Now I visualize the pink blossoms of the chestnut trees and the white marble lace of Fishermen's Bastion up on the hills of Buda lying quiet in the moonlight. I visualize all the beauty of the city I am so fond of, using these memories in a defense against fear.

I talk to God whom I have forgotten over the years.

"Jesus, Son of God, have mercy on us," I pray.

I am not sure if God is listening, but I feel a new strength surging up within me and I finally fall asleep.

* * *

I went up to Irma's apartment to have a bowl of the fantastic soup she prepares daily for everyone, basically made from nothing, a little flour, a few onions and caraway seeds. According to the gossip in the house, Irma was a call girl in Paris many years ago. Now she has a kind, gentle face, and sort of Grandmotherly. Only her eyes gleam now with their old sparkle as she serves the soup with a long wooden spoon. The big iron pot on top of the stove in her kitchen is always full of this good hot soup, as were the wine bottles of Jesus Christ at the marriage in Cana. Her kitchen is full day after day after day with people sitting around everywhere, even on the floor. We eat, and then we discuss the news of the battles on the streets, while Tony, the big, redheaded guy, hands out cigarettes to us, which he stole from the factory where he works. He comes in every day after work, telling us the latest news, his loud voice cheering our spirits.

"There is a rumor that American troops will soon arrive," he says. "The Americans will help us fight the Russians…" His tone of voice is convincing. Everyone including me believes that American troops are just around the corner, that we will have victory over the Soviets and that everything else is a bad dream.

It is so nice to sit here in the warm kitchen having a bowl of soup. It is comforting to hear the murmur of human voices instead of the cannons barking. Or just to stare into nothing, smoking strong cigarettes. It is very very nice. Life is no more than the smoke of a cigarette anyway…

I love the thought that Americans will come and help us. I remember how interesting and handsome the American men looked in the foreign movies. I wonder whether American men are as tall and good-looking and have such excellent teeth as in the movies I used to see with Ester before the war.

* * *

It is the middle of November by now, and nothing has changed except that the continuous broadcasting of the free radio Europe in the hands of freedom fighters has ceased.

A general strike is now taking place in Budapest that includes the railway-men, who are protesting the mass deportation of Hungarian patriots. The strike persists; railroad lines are blown up; attacks are made on the Soviet guards of deportation trains. It is all useless. The trains keep rolling through the countryside during the nights, deporting numbers of men, women, and children (who disappeared into the depth of Siberia or elsewhere, and will never return).

I am confined to my room. Today I heard an unidentified radio station, location unknown. "Soviet soldiers," someone pleaded, "the Hungarian Nation is fighting for freedom. Do not shoot! We will die for our freedom!" The unknown man's voice was clear and bold, and comforted me in my loneliness in the darkness of my room. There is still constant fighting on the streets although the revolution has been crushed. The freedom fighters continue to put up resistance. Today I had a dream. Tibor and I were at our wedding. He smiled at me and bells were ringing. But soon the golds and reds and greens of the summer streets we walked on faded to black and white like the old movies, and I saw him lying in an open coffin. I woke up drenched in perspiration.

I refuse to think that my dream has a meaning; I refuse to think that he is dead or that his bullet-ridden body has been thrown into a ditch. I remember again what he had said last time we were together in his room up on the Hills of Roses, right after he was freed from jail. "You are the light, the blood in my heart, my rainbow after the storm. I'll love you forever."

"Make love to me, my love… please…" I pleaded. I remember I had played this scene once before with Peter. At the same time I felt ashamed to be the one who was begging for love, when that should be the man's perogative. I also remember with aching heart the sadness and disappointment I felt when Peter rejected me, as Tibor rejects me right now. The look in his eyes told me that I was knocking on a tightly closed door, which would not be opened for me at the present time.

I also saw love and pity and sorrow in his eyes.

"We must wait, he said. During times like these there is always a chance one may die. Please be patient, my love. I am dying to have you in my arms… but we must wait… The struggle with the Soviets is not over. I want to marry you with churchbells ringing, flowers everywhere."

"I don't care if I live or die, I want you now," I answered. "It is my weakness that I always fall in love with dedicated men, men with principles. You behave strangely, my love, under the circumstances. Who would believe that nothing happened between us when we are so heavenly alone?"

"You are the puzzle, not me," he said. "I adore your aggressive ways…" He kissed away the tears of disappointment from my eyes, and looked at me with such deep love and joy that I had to cry. The dim room swarmed with particles of brilliant light, whirling like clouds of gnats which were really only the prickles of weariness that swam in the moisture of my eyes. All this was because I had been rejected.

He knew that I was suffering and kissed me with such fervor that my mouth went soft under his and my body limp.

"I am lucky," he said after a while. "The door of darkness has opened and fate let me out into the sun."

Chapter Nine
Eva

EVA, MY COUSIN, ARRIVED this morning. I hadn't seen her for a long time although she was living in Budapest, in a plushy apartment of a member of the secret police whom she had met years ago under strange circumstances. All I knew was that they fell in love and then were always falling in and out of love. I was just about to make some tea for myself when she arrived looking depressed and exhausted, so I offered her some tea too.

"I have lemon," I said, "and a half-loaf of fresh bread and some cheese."

"Thanks, maybe later," she replied. "On my way over, I saw Soviet troops firing on women who were publicly mourning their dead." Eva looked shaken and she sank into an armchair then searched through her blue velvet handbag for a cigarette.

I marveled how strangely beautiful she looked despite her fatigue. She was dressed in a long embroidered skirt, yellow *pufajka*† and long black boots, and she had light blue eyes, pale blue almost like a cat's, and golden hair in long braids. "As you know, I am still the *l'enfant terrible* in my family," she said. "Everyone but you resents me because of Rudi. They can't forgive that I am living with a member of the secret police who is the enemy of the Nation. Now I want to leave him because I am getting tired of him and every damned thing he represents!"

"I am surprised. You were so much in love with him. You know that I don't care who you're living with. You know that!"

"I am definitely leaving the gilded cage," she said. "Absolutely and positively. My eyes are opened. Things are bad now. I often long to cry but I have no tears left. I can't even say that I was victimized it's just that everything is finished on my side now."

"Why don't you love him anymore?"

"What a question!" she said. "How on earth can you ask why one falls in love in the first place?"

"You will feel better when you've told me everything."

She talked the whole afternoon, going back to the time when she first met Rudi and was attracted by his coolness and his good looks, or thought she was. She told me something I already knew about her— that she was attracted to men in uniform— like the time when, at fifteen, she fell in love with the Soviet officer, back in Esztergom.

She told me how her feelings for Rudi had deteriorated over the years. She discovered among other things that he always had other mistresses besides her… mostly young ones.

---

† puffy coat

While Rudi was busy at police headquarters she often went out to fashionable espressos. There, young men and women befriended her, intellectuals who were fed up with Communism and disappointed with its promises and lies. They were planning to escape to the West. There were lawyers and doctors among them, she said, who couldn't practice or get jobs because they came from intellectual families, families not necessarily with money but with a good solid background, and who were the backbones of the country before the Soviet occupation. They came from families where the members attended church on Holidays and Sundays, where mothers and grandmothers taught the children at a very young age how to pray and to respect their elders and love their country. They were nice young people, said Eva, and brought up in the traditional manner and who just couldn't find their place under the false ideologies of Communism. Communism was so alien to Hungarians! So they had decided to escape to the West.

"Many of them had tried before. They were caught and put in jail," she said. "Some of them had been caught more than once. I too became involved, ready to leave any minute. I was fed up with my life. After a lot of preparation we went to the border one day, about six of us. We were desperate to leave. It had become like a fever. We were caught just as we were about to cross the Austrian border— close to freedom. One of the girls was shot dead. I was lucky; I was only sentenced to five years in jail. I was released after two years. It might have been through Rudi's intervention. I'll never really find out. To my surprise he took me back, although he knew that I was a *persona non grata*, and that by taking me back he was jeopardizing his political prestige."

"He must really care for you," I said.

"I don't know, I don't think he does. It was a matter of vanity on his part. He thought himself irresistible. He arranged for one of his girlfriends to give me a ride to police headquarters where I had to report once a week. I was under constant surveillance by the AVH after I was released from jail. I never left the apartment during the day though (people didn't know we were still living together). I would sneak out during the night to get fresh air. Rudi and I fought all the time toward the end. We really hated each other, I think."

"I remember you as being so much in love with him," I said.

"My eyes were opened," she said. "I found out a lot about him. He told me that he had killed quite a few of the young freedom fighters during the revolution. He made no secret of it. He was wounded too during the revolution, and taken to a hospital reserved only for the secret police. Now I was alone, disillusioned and bored. One day when he was in the hospital I looked out of the window and saw a huge crowd on the street, marching. I went out and joined them. They headed toward Republic Square. They told me that the reason for the march was to support a demonstration being held there for the university students who had been arrested the first day of the revolution. They had been taken to the headquarters of the AVH and had not been seen or heard from since. People claimed that they heard strange sounds from underground at the Republic Square, which sounded like muffled screams for help. They heard the sounds every day, day and night, from the time the students vanished."

Eva had grown very pale and tired as she reached this part in her story. I asked her if she would rather not talk about it at all. I tried to change the subject.

"We had so many dreams about life when were were at Grandma's house, remember?" I asked her. It was the wrong question. She started crying.

"I wish I were a child again," she sobbed. "I lived too much and too fast."

"I remember it was summertime and we were on the roof of Grandma's house when you first told me you had a date with a Soviet officer. It was the same day Ester returned from Austria in the wagon."

"Of the three of us, she has done best. She is in love with her husband. I heard she has a happy life. I was only fifteen when I went to bed with the Russian. I didn't really enjoy it, only wanted to hurt myself. When my Mother committed suicide, I was only ten years old. I did stupid things to ease my suffering…"

"I am sorry," I said. "I'll get you a cup of tea, you look very tired."

"Wait," she said. "I must tell you the rest of the story. I must get it out of my system. Perhaps my nightmares will stop if I talk about it…"

She told me that as soon as they reached the Square with the crowd, some of the men had proceeded to dig deep into the ground and uncovered what turned out to be an underground jail connected to the AVH headquarters. The news spread rapidly. The crowd kept shouting, "Let the students free!" Suddenly, the security police began firing into the crowd from the windows of the building, killing and wounding hundreds of people. Tanks arrived from the other end of the Square, flying Hungarian flags. They were the freedom fighters and they were closing in quickly. Following the tanks was a group of people led by a man who carried a huge flag. "Come on! Come on!" he shouted, "The building is ours!" Some of the freedom fighters rushed into the building.

When the AVH men saw that the freedom fighters were safely inside, six of them sauntered out of the building. They were dressed in brand-new uniforms and shiny new boots. They came out laughing, as if it had all been a big mistake, arguing with the freedom fighters and denying they ever tortured prisoners. "Give us a break," they pleaded. Suddenly one of them dropped to the ground and then they all followed, one by one like autumn leaves falling from a tree.

The crowd was silent; there was not even a sigh.

Now a group of policewomen emerged from the building. They were all kicked and spat upon as they passed. A high-ranking officer followed and he also was beaten and kicked. Then his bleeding body was hung from a tree by the feet and men and women spat on him as they passed and cursed him in his death.

When Evi saw the AVH colonel hanging from the tree, she thought about Rudi and felt suddenly sick. She threw up. But the crowd pushed her forward till she was inside the headquarters building and running with the crowd down the stairs. They searched one room after another, trying to find the secret passages, guided by the sounds.

They groped their way into a large bare room that lay in semi-darkness. There they found the corpses, eight of them on the cement floor. Five boys and three girls. Their eyes had been brutally poked out; their faces were turned to the ceiling with a vacant expression. The smell of blood and torn flesh was everywhere and someone in the crowd began to cry. People exclaimed in horror when they saw the walls where breasts and tongues and penises were nailed above the heads of the corpses. Wax-colored breasts and penises and greyish tongues.

The strange sounds from under the ground continued to be heard even after the students' corpses were found— They seemed like inarticulate cries for help.

"They never found the rest of the students. They may still be trapped in some other rooms," said Eva. "They will never be found."

"I feel sick. I can't believe it… Those poor kids. Oh Jesus!"

"I feel sick myself. The secret police. Savage beasts. Worse than animals. I can't sleep; I can't eat. I used to love boiled meat, the kind of which trembles on the plate like the multifold skirts of the peasant girls. Now I can't even look at meat— those greyish penises and tongues pinned to the walls took away my appetite, for good…"

"You must erase it from your mind. Remember Grandma? Remember how strong she was? She was our heroine, do you remember?"

"She is dead. So is my Mother. I have no one. And now Rudi. I want to leave him. I despise him, his profession— everything."

"Stay with me." I asked her. "You can sleep on the couch."

"What about you?"

"I'll put the two big armchairs together. Like we used to do at Grandma's house, on the big holidays, when someone was sleeping in each corner…"

"I want to stay with you, I hope I won't be a nuisance…"

"Why are you blushing again?"

"It is strange," she said. "What am I making such a fuss? We are family. I know that you love me. I feel ill, I am not at peace…"

"No, no, it was a good thing you came. After dinner we will talk. I must tell you about Tibor…"

We talked until dawn, which came fast, as if tired of waiting.

Chapter Ten
IBI

DECEMBER 5, 1956. Today I went to see Ibi, a teenage girl who lives in a small flat belonging to Ada and Nesti, two elderly Jewish ladies who took her in after she lost her father. She has no family now; her mother died a long time ago. We all take care of her. The tenants in the house shower her with food and small gifts. Ibi had fought against the Soviets with a group of other teenagers at an industrial center at the outskirts of Budapest, which is called Red Csepel because it was the home of those hard-core Communist workers who were the most trusted in the regime. A few weeks ago the children of the Communist workers were involved in battles with the Soviets. They fought against them with such fervor that it surprised both the Free World and the U.S.S.R. Ibi and her friends, about seven of them, spread a liquid soap solution on the street, so when two Soviet tanks came along, they spun out of control and hit a building sideways. The children then ambushed the tanks with the Soviet soldiers in them by darting out of doorways and sticking lead pipes into the tanks to make them jam. Then they blew up the tanks with Molotov cocktails.

Two other Soviet tanks drove up and retaliated by firing cannon and machine guns point-blank at the youngsters, wounding and killing many of them. Ibi's cousin, a twelve-year-old boy, ran into the path of the lead tank in the column, a grenade tied to his belt, and blew the tank and himself to pieces. As she watched it all, Ibi stood frozen for a second, then such rage rose in her heart that she darted toward the monstrous Soviet tank, which skidded on the soap and ran into a wall. Her companions and she blew it all to hell. Her father rushed to their aid from another street where the adults had been fighting. He was shot, and fell. Ibi dragged him into a doorway and laid him gently on the stones of the courtyard within.

He lay there in a pool of blood, which oozed into the cracks around the stones. His face was the color of wax as he urged his daughter and other teenagers to leave before the full rage of the Soviets descended on them and they were captured and liquidated.

The siege was momentarily over outside and the youngsters spent the rest of the day in a demolished barrack. Then at dawn they left, creeping through a sewer pipe, and went to a district relatively free of Soviets.

Ibi loves to read history books, so I bought her *Quo Vadis* by Sienkiewicz, hoping that she would be interested in comparing the two dictators who brought so much misery to earth, Kruschev and Nero. Ibi laughed a lot while I was with her and gorged herself on candy. I thought she resembled a fragile china doll with her ivory skin and black braids, until

I looked into her eyes that showed an extraordinary burning intensity.

Chapter Eleven
RAYS OF HOPE

THE FIRST DAYS OF DECEMBER the streets of Budapest were full of cold sunshine, an ice blue, glass-like sky lay over the city. On one relatively calm day, Evi and I went for a walk, jumping across the potholes in the sidewalk and tasting on the tip of our tongues the fresh wind from the direction of Buda. We walked toward the Western Railroad Terminal where only a month before the battles had raged with such force. Now the streets were packed with people, and tents had sprung up on the sidewalks, like giant mushrooms after rain. Inside the tents, people were selling candles, matches, cigarettes and canned food— at outrageous prices.

"I like to see our city so determined to survive," said Evi. "Yet I don't think I will stay in Budapest very long. At the first opportunity, I will seize the chance to follow the white Danube— to Vienna."

When we arrived home, a man was waiting for me in the dark lobby.

"My name is Mihaly Nagy," he said. "I have just arrived from Vienna." He handed me a small package, which I opened with wildly pounding heart. Inside I found a couple of oranges and bananas and a letter from Tibor.

> My Darling, my only love, I am in Vienna, arrived five weeks ago after losing the battles with the Soviets. I had no choice but to escape after learning that the reorganized secret police were already looking for political prisoners with the intention of taking us back to jail. I rode my bicycle all the way to the border, then went by train to Vienna. In Hungary I encountered Soviet troops, yet managed to slip through the lines. I am sending Mihaly, because I want him to help you to leave Hungary. Please trust him, as you would me. Come before it is too late! Come before the electric wires are restored again around Hungary… I dream of you every night. Love forever, Tibor

"I know the secret roads leading to the border by heart," said Mihaly. "They are mostly small deserted roads through the forests." He told us that he was going in and out of Vienna on missions helping the families who had been separated during the revolution to be united again. "And lovers too…" he added and smiled at me reassuringly.

I trusted him completely. He had the self-confident eyes of a Swiss mountain climber.

"I will be back in a few days," he told me, "which gives you enough time to get ready for the journey. In the meantime I will be on another trip across the border, to help a pregnant woman and her mother to get out."

He left and we were never to see him again.

A week later I caught sight of his name in the newspaper. He had been taken prisoner on his last trip back from Vienna. The Hungarian secret police executed him.

Chapter Twelve
THE ESCAPE

"I STILL HAVE THE ADDRESS of the peasant guide who helped me to the border during my ill-fated escape," said Evi. "It wasn't his fault that I was caught. We could take the train to the village where he used to live, close to the Western border."

"I am ready to leave," I told her. "But I think we must include Miriam and her sons. She wants to go so desperately. She talks about it all the time. She feels there is no future for her here, or for her boys."

The most difficult part was to tell mother about my decision. Yet she took the news surprisingly well and calmly. "God help you on your journey," she said, tears welling up in her eyes. "We will meet again some day, somewhere."

I wasn't prepared for the pain I was to suffer in the future in thinking of my mother left behind, alone in the house, and an easy target for the secret police because she had a daughter who had defected to the West.

* * *

By the middle of December about 10,000 people had already left Hungary, taking advantage of the fact that the Communist Government was not yet strong enough to rebuild the iron curtain along the border, with its electric barbed wire, its watchtowers and minefields.

Miriam and her three sons, Evi and myself, joined the exodus on a cold morning, trudging along the snow-covered streets. Miriam led the way carrying a small Christmas tree, Evi and I had brought bottles of cheap wine to bribe the border guards if necessary. Everyone remembered, from the 1945 invasion, that the Soviets had a weakness for booze. They were known to drink anything that contained alcohol, including *eau de cologne*. Miriam's sons, Eric, Sam and Laci, brought up the rear chatting all the way to the station where we boarded the train without incident. The compartments of the train were packed with people; the strong smell of unaired winter coats and body sweat hung in the air. We found a place to sit before the train pulled out.

I stared out of the window and counted the trees, which seemed to run backwards, and I tried not to pay attention to the other people, who sat in their seats tense and unusually quiet.

I was thinking about Mother, who was probably still leaning against the wall, listening to the echo of our departing footsteps, and trying not to cry.

After a while, I grew aware of a rising commotion around me, people jumping out of their seats and gesticulating. I heard someone say that a group of secret police was in the next car, checking travel permits. Through the glass door of my compartment I could see the soldiers with machine guns on their shoulders. One of them with a red face and a thick neck had just finished checking the papers of one woman. Then I saw his hands turn the doorknob, my eyes glued to the fleshy fingers that resembled snakes. Panic was rising within me. Everything had been so well planned, I thought— the Christmas tree for example, to look as though we were visiting grandma in the country. It might now have all been useless.

I suddenly heard Miriam's oldest son, Laci, say, "We must jump off the train! We don't have the necessary travel papers."

Then everything happened very fast, in a matter of seconds. By incredible luck, the train slowed down for a station. Shoving each other we were able to jump off the slowly moving train. We ran breathlessly into the December twilight. While I was running for my life, I heard the cries of the people behind us who got caught as they leapt from the train. I heard the loud curses of the soldiers and looking back I saw bright searchlights scanning the entire area. There was a dirt road ahead of us, lined with bushes and trees. I ran blindly into its blessed darkness, my heart racing wildly, trying to keep up with Miriam and her sons, and Evi. Our luck held. The soldiers didn't follow us into the forest, as they were afraid of a confrontation with the village guerillas.

But darkness was falling on us fast. We ran for a while; then I heard the clucking of chickens, the flutter of their wings, the barking of a dog— and then I saw the amber light of a house…

Soon we staggered blindly into a typical village kitchen. A farm family was having supper round a wooden table lit only by a kerosene lamp. The family consisted of a middle-aged man and his wife, two flaxen-haired young daughters, and a grandmother. They didn't seem surprised to see us or to hear us ask whether we could stay the night. They told us that almost every night refugees knocked on their door. "Our village is very close to the Austrian border," said the farmer, a thin unshaven man with a bent back. His wife laid more plates round the table and offered us some of the bean soup, black bread and milk that they were having. We ate under the ever-watchful eye of the Hungarian poodle that sat in front of the tiled stove in the corner. It was heated with coal and spread heavenly warmth through the room. After supper we asked the farmer if he would be able to help us get to the border. He said he knew a well-known guide in the neighborhood and he sent one of his daughters to fetch him. The young girl returned with the man with a strong jaw, a pug nose, and small piercing eyes like black buttons.

After some negotiation we agreed on a sum of money for his services. When we told him that we had very little money with us, he replied, "You can give me some jewelry instead…" Without hesitation, Miriam took off her wedding ring. As he stood there waiting as if he wanted more, I gave him the only jewelry I had with me, a silver crucifix my mother brought to me from Florence. Evi took the thick gold choker from her neck, and as he still stood waiting, she gave him her ruby earrings. He promised he would return early in the morning to pick us up, and left. We spent the night in the so-called "best" room, which traditionally didn't have any heat and was used mainly for the storage of food, like a pantry… and to display some expensive furniture.

There was a beautifully carved "credence table" covered with china in the room, and two heavy oak beds piled high with embroidered pillows and thick eiderdowns piled up to the ceiling. In the room also hung some headcheese and smoked ham and long sausages on a thick rope, along with two brand-new lambskin coats.

This farmer must have quite a lot of money, I thought, judging by the furnishings and the quantity of food in the house. Almost everyone in the country was suffering from some kind of shortage. Unable to sleep, freezing even under the heavy quilts, I lay listening to the strange silence of the forest outside the windows.

Then I heard Evi say, "The logical thing would be to walk to the border during the night. Why does he want us to go by daylight? We'll be an easy target for the border guards."

"Try not to worry!" I answered. "The man must know his business. We are not the first he has guided to the border, you heard him…"

"He said he'd help us; we have to trust him," broke in Miriam from the other bed where she slept with her sons. "Say your prayers and try to sleep…"

* * *

The sun was already rising as we followed our guide through the forest and left the whitewashed houses of the village behind. The scene was bathed in a soft red light from the rising sun. After some time we reached a crossroads and, choosing one of the two ways, we left the forest and entered a flat plateau where a yellow station house stood at a distance. Our guide stopped suddenly. "Continue your way alone." He pointed toward the yellow house. "Go directly through the station house. The other side is Austrian territory and the first Austrian village is only a few miles off." He turned and quickly left us.

We walked through the abandoned building as if in a trance. On the other side we walked straight into the arms of a group of Soviet and Hungarian soldiers who waited there armed with machine guns. A Soviet-made truck was parked at the edge of the wheat field already packed with other refugees.

"Get into the truck!" shouted one of the soldiers who had narrow slits for eyes. The people on the benches of the truck looked defeated, like animals on the way to the slaughterhouse. What we couldn't understand was that the truck did not move for several hours. We kept wondering whether the soldiers were waiting for other refugees to come through the station house. In the meantime, the sky became cloudy and an icy rain began to fall.

One of the soldiers threw a tarpaulin canvas over the truck above our heads, and the outside world was shut out. Many children were among the group, and one small girl kept throwing up and asking her mother the same question over and over: "Mother, what will happen to us? Why are they keeping us?"

We waited for a couple of hours while more people kept arriving and being pushed into the truck.

Finally, we were on our way, destination unknown. We rode for a long time, and then the truck came to a stop and we were ordered to get out. In front of us stood a building that looked like a military barrack, lonely and bleached by the eerie light of the moonless sky. Only the backdrop of the purple-colored forest softened its bleak silhouette.

The guards led us inside along an endless corridor. The huge room we entered was packed with people, the tired faces of hopelessness and desperation.

About a dozen policewomen were in waiting for us, their faces waxy and full of shadows beneath the naked light bulbs. They guided us to the far end of the room where a long wooden table was set with tin cups and plates. The walls around the tables were splattered with food thrown there in disgust by some rebellious refugee.

"Eat your soup and bread!" blared the loudspeaker. "When you have finished dinner each of you will be assigned to a separate room for questioning."

I gazed at the row of brown doors that stood between me and the sinister secrecy of the rooms behind them, and I wondered what would become of me once I got inside. Then I slowly ate the tepid soup and stale bread and listened wearily to the loudspeakers, which never ceased from blaring. They played a song that had been specially selected for the occasion by the secret police.

> I wish I was home again. I wish I could see my homeland— the beautiful evenings full of the magic rays of moon. The geraniums on my mother's windowsills. Oh, how I wish to see

> my homeland again. My homeland is the only place in the world to find joy.

I watched in horror while people disappeared one by one behind the doors. And I waited for my turn.

"Room three," said the policewoman. "It's your turn to go."

The room I entered was decorated with red flags and with the usual photographs of Marx and Lenin who fixed me with their piercing eyes.

"Have a seat," said the AVH man.

He sat behind a huge desk, and while he spoke in the soft voice of one suggesting a rendezvous, he looked at me in a cold rage. His eyes were colorless behind his glasses. He talked to me for a long time while I stared down the cavernous depth of his throat as he opened his mouth to repeat over and over, mercilessly, "Why did you do it? Were you hoping for a better life? Where? Why? Why? Why?"

Suddenly, I was afraid no longer. "You know exactly why…" I said. "For the same reason that everyone else is leaving. I am fed up with everything— with the promises, with the lies…"

I told him things I wouldn't have dared to say under any other circumstances. Or if I had— I would have gone to jail sure as hell.

Suddenly, he burst out like a volcano. "Like rats…" he shouted! "Like rats from a sinking ship. You run away, all of you! But the ship is not sinking as you all think. You got caught up in the hysteria of the masses! I advise you! I warn you! If we ever catch you again, you will be put away for years."

After a while he regained his composure and suppressing his anger he said, "We will let you go this time. You will be taken back to Budapest with the trucks tomorrow morning."

You don't have enough room in your jails right now, I thought. You don't have room for the thousands and thousands of people caught at the border at present. So don't try to give me the impression of generosity. You are a pig, I thought, but I kept silent.

He wrote my name and address into a big black book, and looked at me once more, the muscles twitching round his thin, tense lips. "You can leave the room," he said coldly.

I left with my head held as high as when I entered. I found Miriam anxiously waiting outside, pale and worried.

"What is it?" I asked her and somehow I knew the answer, in my heart…

"They took her away, two mean-looking policewomen. They led her away after the interrogation…" she said.

"Poor Eva, my poor, poor cousin…" I cried. "Was it Rudi, was he her interrogator?"

"He was, he was," she said, her eyes full of tears. "She managed to speak to me, a few words. She sends you her love and she asks you to pray for her."

We slept a few hours, resting our heads on our elbows and leaning across the table. It wasn't very easy to sleep so near to the incessant blaring of the loudspeakers. Besides, Eva was on my mind all the time. She was on my mind, she was on my mind…

* * *

I think about Eva now all the time, vividly recalling the time when we were young. While Grandma was still living, Uncle Demeter would often invite us to his old country house in Transdanube to celebrate the grape harvest. The last time we were there Eva was about fourteen years old, resplendently beautiful, daring like a young huntress. She was everywhere that day, watching Lina and old Demeter roasting the pig before the open fire early in the morning (the moon was still up on the sky) then helping to press the luscious clusters of Riesling and golden-eyed assu grapes, dancing with her bare feet inside a huge barrel, while the sweet juice of the grapes dripped into the wooden tub.

I, too helped to press the grapes, we sang old folk songs, our voices carried lightly down to the valley by the fragrant autumn wind. Later in the afternoon, we stole down to a cellar cut deep into the side of the mountain, to take part in a "romantic experience" as Eva called it.

The two young peasant boys with whom we flirted during the day followed us there. We kissed behind the barrels, which were filled with cool old wine, surrendering to the warmth of tradition as deeply rooted as the wine. The peasant boys were good looking, their bodies as strong as the new branches of the poplar trees. They teased us with words and we laughed and laughed. Life was full of laughter and happiness and with the fragrance of our young bodies.

I want to remember Eva as she was on that particular day, gay and happy and beautiful… always. I want to keep her intact in my mind. She was like the new blossom of an apple tree. I want to erase from my mind the memory of the day she hanged herself in the jail. She took her life in her own hands, just as her mother had done years before.

I remember reading somewhere that the seeds of what we do in our own lives are in all of us…

Chapter Thirteen
THE SECOND ESCAPE

BUDAPEST LOOKED DESOLATE as we returned by truck the next day. I made my way on foot through the silent, devastated early-morning streets toward home, my footsteps ringing on the broken sidewalks.

Mother wasn't home. I called the hospital and learned that she had been sent to another hospital where she was especially needed. I was glad that she wasn't home, because I was determined to try to escape again, and I didn't want her to go through the excruciating pain of saying goodbye to each other again. I barely had time to fix myself a cup of tea when there was a knock on the door. Olga, the big shot in the Communist party came in, she lived on the third floor and had been assigned to the house by the secret police to keep informed of the political beliefs of the tenants. One of her duties was to report to the AVH who among those tenants could be trusted or not trusted from the Party's point of view. She came in looking like a walking question mark.

"I've been looking for you for about two days," she said. "Where have you been?"

"At Grandma's house, in Esztergom," I lied. "I was invited by Aunt Maria who still lives there, you know, for the preparation of the holidays."

"A lot of people in the house are playing with the notion of leaving, getting on," she said.

"Can you read people's minds? How did you find out? Why would they want to leave?" I asked her, my heart contracting.

"We have ways of getting even with the relatives who are left behind," she said, and her voice was almost gentle, but her eyes sent out flashes of lightning.

"Oh well, that doesn't apply to me," I said, trying to be nonchalant while my heart pounded from fear for my mother's safety. Everyone knew Olga, everyone in the big apartment house feared her. People knew about her devotion to the Party and also about her big love affair with Kalimov, the Soviet General. The affair had ended years ago, the General being ordered back to Kiev to his children and to his wife. He vanished out of Olga's life as if by magic. Yet the flaming melodies, the loud music still could be heard from her flat, those strange and halting rhythms of Stravinsky, the long, vehement and ethereal music of Tchaikovsky, the mordant, sad and sinister compositions of Rimsky Korsakov. The melodies were heard from her room mainly on those occasions when she had to report someone in the house to the secret police. She got satisfaction and special pleasure and joy in this way, I imagined.

"I have a headache, I don't feel well," I complained and observed that she remained stubborn as a mule, standing in the doorway. She kept staring at me and she kept repeating sentences like "I still say that people in the house are considering leaving Hungary." She spoke very loud and indignantly. Finally she left looking like a monument to suspicion, and murmuring something like "...the pigs, the rotten pigs, enemies of the People's Republic, every one of them."

Enlightened, I turned the radio on. I tuned in to Radio Free Europe and later on to Voice of America hoping that I could hear something interesting.

"We are in Vienna," I heard, "sheltered and fed by the American Red Cross, feeling happy and excited and well! We'll be going to America as soon as we get visas. Wish you were here with us…"

It was the voices of refugees who had already arrived in Austria. Their voices were full of life and poured into the silence of my room leaving a taste like bittersweet chocolate bonbons to whet my appetite. I'll get to Vienna even if I have to walk through icy rivers or climb mountains, at any price, I said to myself.

* * *

The early-morning sky was covered with grey snow clouds as we climbed down from the truck after the long exhausting trip from Budapest. All along the way, the roads had swarmed with military police checking each vehicle in search of refugees. Luckily, we remained undetected by hiding behind two big barrels on the truck with a Soviet license plate, and the customary red star painted on the front. The fact that our driver looked very "Russian" also helped our situation. He was a big man with watery blue eyes, small pug nose and Slavic features, and spoke fluent Russian. He was equipped with all the necessary documents including the reason for his "business trip": to obtain a cow at the request of his boss, the Soviet captain. Our driver's name was Laci. We had met him a few days before in a pub on Nefelejcs Street after we had had an unsuccessful shopping trip to the city in search of food. We had stood in line in front of the stores, but when our turn finally came, the shelves of the store were completely empty. We couldn't even buy a loaf of bread, Miriam and I.

Exhausted, we felt like having a glass of beer, which we were certain we could buy. So we entered a pub that was packed with people drinking and gossiping, the whole place looking more like a market than a pub. There were big tables along the walls loaded with boxes of eggs, flour, butter, potatoes and fresh vegetables, salami and sticks of kolbasz, and chickens tied together in pairs clucking loudly underneath the table. There in the midst of this hustle and bustle and cacophony stood Laci, looking like Neptune rising from the sea but surrounded with people. When Miriam saw him she was overjoyed. It turned out they knew each other well. He was an old acquaintance of hers.

They exchanged hugs and kisses and I was introduced. Then the three of us went to the back room where he ordered a hot meal and drinks for us, and where we could talk undisturbed.

He talked about his fairly new job at the Soviet Headquarters where he was hired as a purchasing agent and was responsible for supplying all the food. "I stop here every

Wednesday to do business," he said. "I sell food to anyone who comes in— with only a very small profit for myself."

"I knew right away that you were up to something… the minute I saw you," said Miriam.

"I make very little money at the Headquarters," he said. "Besides, the proprietor allows me to do this and instead of paying for his own purchases he gives me a few bottles of rum. This I present to the Soviet captain who is feeling a little frightened and insecure in this strange city. With the help of the rum he gains a feeling of security and everyone is happy. I feel important being able to fill the stomachs of the people. As for the number of missing boxes, the captain makes a little adjustment in his books— no problem."

We told him about our ill-fated escape and capture.

"God sent you here," he said. "It was His will for us to meet. Listen! I know a farmer in a village where I must go in a couple of days to buy a cow for the Soviet captain. The young peasant can take you to the Austrian border. He is a poor fellow who needs the money to buy food for his family, for his infant son. So get as much money together as you can and get ready for the trip."

"You are a smart Catholic but you have the brains of a Jew!" said Miriam. "Jehovah must love me to give me a friend like you," she added.

As the outcome of that discussion, two days later we arrived at a small house that stood at the edge of the village. Its windows were stuffed with straw and a thin smoke rose from its chimney. Inside a young couple greeted us with the traditional politeness of the Hungarian peasant, offering us some milk and bread before we began negotiating.

The young farmer named Imre was a sad-looking man dressed in an old military jacket. He looked worn-out, hungry, and disillusioned like one who is unable to provide his family with even the barest essentials. When we had arrived at a mutual agreement, he told us we would start our journey after sunset.

"Don't go, Imre!" his young wife cried desperately.

"You know well we need the money," he answered laconically, his eyes focusing on the peeling walls. He looked 'round the kitchen which was barren and cold like the colorless garden and the muddy roads outside.

"You will get caught like your brother!" she cried. "You don't even know if he is alive!"

After a few hours of sleep, huddled together on the floor in front of the kitchen stove, we prepared for the trip. We left the house and, at the front gate, Imre kissed the soft damp hair of his infant son who was held in the arms of his wife. She stood there in despair until we were out of sight.

In order not to attract the attention of the Soviet T-34 tanks that patrolled the area outside the forest, we walked in deep silence. Imre told us we would walk fifteen kilometers for three consecutive nights in the forest and we would get some sleep during the days at the homes of some of his friends.

In the immeasurable darkness and the cotton-like fog, I began to feel slightly claustrophobic as the hours went by.

Imre walked ahead of us holding his axe. Miriam following with the rigid posture of someone resigned to fate.

The grey lights of dawn appeared above the trees after we had walked about eight hours and finally stopped at a little rundown house hidden behind a dilapidated stone wall. Here we spent the day sleeping like logs, on a blanket laid along the wall, in the badly heated kitchen where the walls were as cold as the marble headstones of a cemetery in wintertime. We went to sleep without eating any breakfast. The morose old peasant couple couldn't offer us anything having next to nothing for themselves.

We woke up at suppertime to find the table set, a jug of milk, some bread, and a few apples smiling at us.

"I bought them in the village," said Imre. "Please eat fast. Then we must continue on our way right after dusk."

We had walked only a few hours when he suddenly stopped.

"Hide behind the trees!" he ordered. He himself stayed in the clearing grasping his axe.

I peeked out from behind the trees and saw some shadows moving in the darkness, their feet making crunching sounds on the snow left over from the last snowfall a few days before.

My body was covered with perspiration in spite of the cold wind, my heart raced.

I hoped that the approaching shadows were not the border guards. I prayed. A thin moon appeared between two clouds and illuminated the landscape. Then I saw them clearly. They were refugees like us: men, women, and children. When we emerged from behind the trees, they scattered in all directions. Later when the confusion was cleared up we all laughed hysterically at the humor of the situation, refugees scaring refugees.

Then we all walked together on the endless paths of the forest, our shadows merging with the shadows of the trees.

We got to know the newcomers who consisted of a young couple, both medical doctors; an older woman and her three granddaughters; and a young woman writer with a five-year-old, blue-eyed girl, named Rita. They had become lost in the forest in their attempt to get to the border on their own. And they were indeed glad to join our group.

At the break of the second dawn we arrived at a house standing proudly on a small hill.

"This house once belonged to the village doctor, a Jew who was burned to ashes together with his family in Auschwitz," said Imre. "It has been mostly vacant since the family was driven away on the highway," he continued. "It's been ransacked several times by some of the villagers, looted by the Soviet soldiers during the war. The village people loved the old doctor, his gentle wife and their two pretty waxen-faced daughters. They grieved when the family died. Sometime later a newcomer to the village, the Communist secretary and his wife came to live here. They loved the long rows of rooms inside and the elaborate garden, and they were planning to stay here for good.

But one day the wife of the secretary was drawn to the window by a strange noise. There in the eerie light of the early spring dusk, she saw the "dead" doctor, his wife, and the two girls swaying in the deck chair… back and forth… back and forth…

"After seeing the ghosts and not being able to rationalize what she had seen, the wife of the Party secretary slowly lost her mind. Being a convinced atheist, she believed neither in God nor in life after death. No, she didn't believe that 'nonsense' as she told the people who paid her visits at the insane asylum where she was confined soon after the incident."

"It is an interesting story," I said to Imre when he finished with the tale of the house. "I love thrillers… and I really don't feel sorry for the wife of the Party secretary. I think I sympathize more with the ghosts," I said. Ghosts or no ghosts, I loved the once elegantly furnished and now barren rooms in which we all slept on the floor under the red velvet draperies on the French windows, bled of their color over the years. While we slept, Imre must have gone out to buy some food and brought back a loaf of bread (stale), a jar of sauerkraut and two dead pigeons from which we made delicious soup. He also returned with some bad news.

"I can't guide you any farther," he said.

He explained to us that in the village he had met one of his friends who was a native of that village and home on leave from the jail where he was warden.

"He is a warden at the jail where my brother is held," he said. "My brother has been in jail since last month when he was caught guiding refugees across the border. Now I'm told he is very, very sick. I must go to see him. I must try…"

He said he had already hired another guide for us and made arrangements for us to meet him in the forest at midnight.

After saying an emotional goodbye to him, he left us reluctantly and headed toward the village.

It seemed like forever as we waited behind a big rock as he had instructed us. It was long past midnight and we had almost given up hope, when we finally heard a whistle come through the darkness. As arranged, we returned the signal to identify ourselves.

A young man drew near, thin, dark, and tense like a hunting dog, clad in a worn out jacket and heavy boots, armed with an axe.

They are coming out of the woodwork, these hungry and pathetic figures, risking their lives for a little money, I thought. How brave they are! How daring!

What a fruitless life they must have in this Communist paradise, their families starving and in rags. What a hopeless life they must lead to be ready and willing to face danger and death in order to make a small amount of money under the most hazardous circumstances.

He was the same type of person as Imre… he radiated trustfulness.

"Soon we will be leaving the forest," he said, "and we'll continue our way through an open field. I can't warn you enough of the danger we face. The field outside the forest is swarming with tanks hunting for refugees… with T-34s…"

A few hours later we said goodbye to the forest and emerged on an open snowfield where at the far end of the horizon we could see the faint blue crests of the Alps. We had to continue our journey without the blessed shelter of the trees. It wasn't long before we heard the metallic rumbling of the caterpillars. Within seconds the long orange tongue of a military flare lit up the area and the sky.

"On the snow! Quickly!" commanded our guide.

I threw myself on the ground. I tried to make myself as flat and invisible as possible. I lay on the snow numb like a rabbit, pretending to be dead under the frightening glare while my heart pounded.

It happened again and again! The flares! Then it was dark again… blessed darkness. Then suddenly the flares would go up again into the sky, painting the faces of the children with an orange glow. Then the snow began to fall and fell with full force, beautifully designed crystal flakes that glowed with the faint purple color of amethysts.

We dragged our feet one after another in the deepening snow like automatons, numb from exhaustion. The dark figures of people staggering in the snow reminded me of a dance scene celebrating some terrible event at a finale from an opera.

"We must walk faster!" said our guide. "We must reach the river long before dawn."

Rita, the little girl, said she had to pee. "Mommy, I can't hold it anymore!" I heard her desperate cry.

Her mother hurried up to the guide who walked in front holding his axe. She asked him if we could stop for a minute.

"Not just now! Not even for a minute!" was his answer. "We must get to the river while the Americans are still there, before morning comes."

"You must pee as we walk, honey," I heard the mother say to the child.

Her pee left a small dark trail in the snow; her pants froze and stuck to her legs in the cold wind.

Later on, Miriam's oldest son lost one of his shoes in the snow and we didn't have time to look for it. So he continued the journey hopping on one leg like a wounded bird.

I felt very tired. It would be nice to lie down in the snow, I thought. The landscape began to twist and bend before my eyes. I felt faint.

"Hang on!" I heard someone saying. "It can't be too far!"

There must be lights and houses at the other end of the darkness I thought. There must be houses at the other end of the snowfields with lighted windows. I must collect all my strength to get there. Tibor is waiting in Vienna, I must be strong and brave.

I heard Mrs. Puskas breathing hard as she walks behind me. She is finding it difficult to walk in the deepening snow. I hear her saying, "Help! Someone help me, please!" The tone of her voice sounds desperate. I turn around to see what is wrong, and then I see her falling. She falls in a grotesque way like a bag full of potatoes, ungracefully… fatally.

Suddenly, everyone surrounds her… the doctor and his wife are administering mouth-to-mouth resuscitation. In vain.

"She is dead!" declares the doctor. It is a terrible shock to everyone, but because we are numb we don't feel the shock so deeply. It stays somehow on the surface of our emotions.

Her granddaughters are the ones who really feel the pain of her death. They are crying uncontrollably. The guard is nudging us. We must continue on our way. We can't even stop to bury her so we must leave her in the snow. There is a commotion. The girls refuse to leave their grandmother. Her stiffening body is already taking on the condition of rigor mortis. We all throw a handful of snow over her… and convince the girls to continue the journey. "It is better this way," says Miriam. Mrs. Puskas confessed to me that she was a member of the Party. She could probably never get to America. They don't give visas to Communists, I hear."

"I can understand that," I answer. "I can quite understand the Americans, can't you?"

"Definitely!" says Miriam. "Communists and Nazis… they brought suffering to the world. In 1944, when the Jews tottered along the snowfields driven by the Nazis, the roads were edged with corpses. We are lucky that we only have one dead behind us!"

There comes a moment when one gives up hope, when the body and soul refuse to help each other in the struggle to survive, and the only solution for the absolute despair which invades the person like a terminal illness is the wish to die!

Mrs. Puskas' death must be taking its toll. I find myself wishing I could be in her place stretched out on the snow. I am completely numb, body and spirit. I am exhausted beyond words.

It is true that I have never been very strong, at least not the last couple of years. I have been suffering from malnutrition; my nerves are on the verge of breaking as the result of the crowded living condition in Budapest since the Soviet occupation. The prescribed barbiturates and sleeping pills I took only masked the symptoms. They did not help.

I pray to God to help us reach the border and to let the American students be there on the Austrian side as our guide has promised.

While I am occupied with my gloomy and negative thoughts, absorbed in my last dark and nihilistic viewpoint, I haven't noticed that we have already left the snowfields and are continuing our way on a narrow path lined with winter shrubs.

All of a sudden, I am aware of some turbulent excitement all round me. People are whispering and gesticulating and pointing toward something in the distance with muffled cries.

"The River!" I hear them saying. "The River! The River!"

Then I see it for myself. It doesn't look like a river, but rather like a canal with its muddy dark water billowing and a muddy bank edging it on each side. In either case, river or canal, my heart beats, loudly like a drum. I am hilariously happy to see it! It's certainly the most thrilling and glorious sight I've seen in a long time.

Thank God we made it, I say to myself. God bless our guide and the whole world!

We have arrived at our destination and a whole brand-new world is waiting, where there will be no more hunger and humiliation, no more Soviet tanks and soldiers and secret police, no more barbed wire or police dogs. Perhaps there is a little corner of the world waiting where we can live in peace and in dignity, where we don't have to live like slaves in our own land. I am anxious to see the Americans who wait across the river every night for refugees like us coming out of the dark. According to our guide, they will come to get us with a rubber raft if we are lucky.

"Since the exodus began, those American university students are sitting in the dark risking their lives to come to the Hungarian side. They could easily be caught and shot by the border guards," said our guide. Silently I ask God to bless them for being there and coming over to rescue hundreds of people every night. It must be a wonderful country that produces such fine brave men who perform such daring, heroic acts. I strain my eyes searching hard for the Americans through the smoke-colored foliage at the other side, but I can detect no sign of life… *nichts*†… *rien*‡*!* Every one of us is dead tired. We're also tense and frightened because we know how easily we can be discovered by the border guards who search this area when the early light of morning approaches. Just then our anxiety increases as the masses of clouds around the moon are already beginning to clear. Dawn is arriving with light steps.

Our guard is circling with a flashlight to indicate that we are here and then waits for a similar sign signaling that we have been noticed on the other side. There's no response.

---

† nothing
‡ nothing

The children are praying with heads bent and even the landscape seems to hold its breath, waiting. Just when everyone has almost given up hope, suddenly an orange light going in circles appears on the other side.

Just at the same time a transparent light brightens the sky with excessive radiation… the first light of morning.

Shortly afterwards, a rubber raft can be seen gliding towards us in the eerie greyness, coming closer and closer.

All of a sudden I don't feel tired anymore, a lightness comes over me, an almost perfect bliss which would be called by the mystics a "union with God." I am aware of the fact that I am experiencing one of the most thrilling moments of my life that I will remember forever, and will live to tell my grandchildren. I drink in the magnificence of the moment with all my senses, with my eyes and my nerves and with every part of my body, as if I were experiencing the uniqueness of paradise— there where souls are in perfect peace amid the rich colors, the warm browns, the glittery golden lights and the deep jade greens of some ethereal background. I even imagine that I hear the music of the spheres when in reality there is perfect stillness in the air and there is only a grey rubber raft gliding on muddy waters with two young men on board. The snowfields and icy winds and numb days and nights are forgotten. When the Americans come ashore wading through the water with their hip-high boots and grey rain jackets, they actually look like earthlings, while I was expecting something like archangels, or at least someone looking like Nelson Eddie or Tyrone Power, whom I had seen in an American movie long, ago with my grandmother.

Anyway, there is no time to scrutinize them in detail or to appreciate their interesting foreignness. We are ordered to board the raft, women and children first. They promise to return for the men.

Our raft is rapidly pulled to the other side by a thick rope and then it is all over. We are in Austria. Before I set my feet on free land, I look back once more to the land of my childhood, trying to capture something I could save like a treasure for myself. But all I can see is a Communist watchtower looming in the distance. I begin to sob uncontrollably.

After disembarking, we are led to several jeeps waiting for us. I get into one of them with Miriam and her sons.

I can't take my eyes off the driver who drives with an amazing speed despite the bumpy roads. He tells us to call him "Joe" as if we've known him a long time. He is a blonde blue-eyed American with a gleaming smile and a trusting expression on his face. He is the product of the richest continent in the world. Although he has never experienced war on his native soil, he had great empathy for us. He smiles at us reassuringly from time to time, until at last we arrive to a long white building, the local schoolhouse we are told.

Inside the well-heated rooms an army of Red Cross ladies and reporters are waiting for us. The English and German and French voices are assuring us that we are now on the safe side of Europe. There is a lot of hustle and movement in the classrooms that have become a refugee camp. New groups of refugees are arriving. The reporters are swarming. They take pictures of us for all kinds of newspapers around the world. It feels strange to be in the limelight. I am not yet accustomed to the sensationalism of the Western World. I feel uncomfortable under the revealing strobe light and try to cover my face with my hands, my hollow face and unwashed hair.

A young reporter who looks very American with his short-cropped auburn hair is taking pictures of Rita's wet shoes from every angle. Her shoes had become half rotten from walking in the snow. I notice he is watching me from the corner of his eyes. He has yellow-gold eyes. I can see them from here. He comes over to me and asks me if he can take a photograph of me.

"I am Tom Allen, from New York," he introduces himself.

"I am Kinga from Budapest," I say, feeling like a rag doll, limp and untidy in the warm-up suit I've worn day and night for one week. I don't smell like a bouquet of roses either. He speaks fairly good German. Right away he tells me that his ancestors came from Bremenhaven. He is tall and lanky and his eyes are kind and I would love to chat with him under other circumstances. But my only desire now is to take a hot shower and afterwards to sleep… sleep… sleep.

The children have gathered around the decorated Christmas tree. They don't seem to be exhausted anymore, their tiredness evaporated in the lights of the Christmas tree, which stands in full glory in one corner. Each child is clutching a small toy he has been given. My eyes fall on a long table set with a variety of foods, bread and cold cuts and fruit, jugs of coffee and tea. Someone is peeling an orange. Its tangy aroma fills the room.

The scent of citrus fruit and bananas mixed with the smell of colorful new wool blankets piled up in a corner is alluring. I inhale it slowly and luxuriously as the special smell of the new country. (For many years to come, I am to associate that smell with freedom.)

The reporter notices that my attention is focused on the food. Considerately, he guides me to the table and watches me with amusement while I eat like a field worker, devouring sandwich after sandwich. Meanwhile he puffs on his pipe in silence, and I don't even notice when he leaves. There is too much noise and food and distractions in the room. Later someone leads me to the shower room where I feel ecstasy as I stand under the scalding fountains of water. Afterwards, I throw myself on one of the cots along the wall where many people are already sleeping.

Before I sink into a dreamless sleep, the face of the reporter appears before the eyes of my soul like a translucent vision and half consciously I keep wondering, why?

I wake up early in the afternoon to the hullabaloo coming from outside, the whinny of horses and all kinds of German dialects rising from the schoolyard, which seems like a market as I look out from the window. Buggies and horse-drawn carriages are leaving and arriving, people gathering in groups. I don't have time to digest what is going on because a Red Cross lady comes in accompanied by an Austrian farmer family. She is asking me if I would like to join them for the Christmas holidays. The family consists of an old couple and a mother-in-law, who is ninety-five-years old. Her age does not prevent her from driving the wagon with two old warhorses up the macadam road. I accept their invitation and I find out Rita and her mother will also join us. We are the only ones in the room. Everyone has already left with other Austrian families.

On our way we meet other buggies and wagons carrying other refugees. The villages around the area are filled with the clangor of church-bells announcing the arrival of Christmas. I watch with admiration as Grandma holds the reins in her strong old hands… I gaze into the sky that resembles a lake reflecting the silver-colored snow clouds above our heads. We finally arrive at the farmhouse that stands on a hilltop overlooking the local cemetery, ancient headstones standing there covered with sea-colored moss. The house is small, old, and as hunchbacked as our three hosts. (The mountain peasants in Austria are often cripples as a result of intermarriage.)

The kitchen we enter is dark and cold, and it is permeated with the musty odor of old furniture and a long winter. I sit on the bench in front of the tiled fireplace, watching as the dog licks Rita's frostbitten hands and as the women prepare the evening meal. I notice even the dog looks a little strange. One of his eyes is light blue, and the other is flaming violet! Grandma is snapping the scrawny neck of an undernourished hen to be cooked. She lets the blood flow into an iron pot, and then her daughter fries it with onions in hot lard. Irene is helping to bake bread while the farmer brings in freshly milked goat milk. We eat heartily then we gather around and sing O Tannenbaum. The evening is impregnated by the Christmas tree, kindness & goodwill, and the aroma of chicken soup… My heart overflows with gratitude seeing how much these farmers want to please us, open their homes to us, and share the little they have with us!

After supper, Grandma shows us what they call the "clean room" consisting of some rickety furniture and absolutely no heat. She tucks us into the huge oak bed where we all sleep together with our winter coats on. We freeze even under the heavy feather quilt, our feet resting on two hot steaming irons wrapped in towels.

A picture of Saint Sebastian hangs on the peeling wall looking down at us with the long-suffering eyes of a Christian martyr. Some of the village lads are serenading outside, singing Christmas carols beneath our windows, their ringing tenors and mellow baritones mingling with the indignant barking of dogs.

Rita tosses and turns. I noticed earlier that she was a little uncomfortable as she looked at the long thin noses and square jaws of the women of the house and the large mole on the farmer's chin, which certainly didn't make him look an Adonis.

"This is a witch's house, isn't it?" she whispers in the darkness. "What if they poison us with the meals?"

"Nonsense, honey. They're old, but they are wonderful people, and we must be grateful to them for such a nice Christmas," I hear her mother saying. "Now say your prayers and try to sleep!"

I think about my mother, wondering if she is spending Christmas alone. I remember how she used to throw dried pine needles and apple peels in wintertime on top of the stove and how the scent of honey and pine resin transformed our kitchen to an enchanted island. Mother had a special talent for turning ordinary things into special somethings.

When we woke up the next morning. Grandma presented us with the winter pears and gilded nuts that were the only decorations on their Christmas tree. Then we all drove back to the schoolhouse, Grandma sitting in the driver's seat enthroned like a queen.

* * *

"The whole world is waiting to hear anything you have to tell… tell me something about your life in Hungary…" asked the reporter, the one who took pictures of Rita's rotten shoes. (I remember how astonished I was to notice his eyes become moist on seeing the condition those shoes were in. I recall reading in a magazine somewhere that American men never cry.) We were sitting in a restaurant in Eisenstadt where he had driven me in his red Citroen right after we arrived back at the schoolhouse from the farm. It seemed he waited especially for me in the snow-covered yard, his face red from the cold, his smile gleaming with joy as I stepped down from the wagon.

"I asked the Camp director's permission to invite you out to dinner. I hope you will come. I know a nice little restaurant in Eisenstadt. It would give me such pleasure to show you Burgenland," he said.

Although I was surprised at the unexpected invitation, I accepted it without hesitation. The only other Americans I had met were the students who rescued us, so to be his companion and get to know him seemed like an interesting adventure. Besides I was eager for another hot meal. The restaurant was warm and cozy and crowded with local folks, merchants and their pear-shaped wives, taxi drivers, and officers from the garrison in the nearby village. They sat 'round long tables, eating and drinking seriously, the smell of plum schnapps and garlic was overpowering.

"I am not the only one interviewing refugees," Tom Allen said. "One of our best writers, James Mitchener, is here in Austria. He goes every night to the border and waits for people coming out of the dark. He plans to write a book based on their stories, about children who fought with Molotov cocktails, housewives who seized arsenals. He thinks that your revolution will have a lasting impact even on the Soviets."

"There isn't much to tell you. I existed, and that's about it!" I say when he asks about my life during the Soviet invasion of Hungary. "I never got out of the country. The iron curtain is real. There are electric wires all around the border. But almost every night I traveled in my dreams. I had one recurrent dream— going on a train toward the ocean. On each occasion the train got lost in the dense fog on the winding tracks. I was desperate to get there. I have never seen the ocean. I used to taste the name of the ocean on my lips. Tell me please, how does the ocean look?"

"Breathtaking," he said. "It changes its colors according to the sky, sometimes it is delicate blue, sometimes cobalt blue, silver green, but most of the time it is just beautiful blue like your eyes. What would you like to have for dessert?"

"Apple strudel and a glass of milk."

"You come from a different world. I've never met a girl like you," he said.

"Maybe I have the stigma of a slave on me, coming from Communist Hungary. Otherwise I can't see why I should be different… I can tell you though, my spirit is free. There is no way that the spirit could be exploited, only the body. I used almost everything to distract myself from the dullness and greyness of Communism. One learns how to enjoy things like the drama of the sunset, the whisper of the rain. A terrific book can take away the sadness, and also good music. I prefer classical music. The *ne plus ultra* to being distracted is to fall in love. In Budapest love was the main topic…" He looked at me attentively, his eyes sympathetic without being intrusive.

"I am trying to analyze it. It could be a mixture of innocence and erotica, naivety and knowing it all. You are definitely different from anyone I have met before."

The waitress who looked like a spring bouquet in her embroidered dirndl brought a mug of milk and two slices of hot, vanilla-scented strudel. The old waiter, looking like an aging altar boy in his white apron, brought a bottle of Moselblumchen. Then he went behind the counter and changed the dial on his radio. Berlin came in, someone broadcasting the news; then a woman sang Schubert's Ave Maria from Roma. He changed his dial again— station Paris came in— someone playing a piano concerto, the Liebesträume of Franz Liszt, filling the room with desire.

"It is beautiful music. It fits the occasion," Tom said.

He didn't explain any further so I wasn't sure what he meant by that. He kept looking at me in a certain way.

He is so different from European men, I thought, and certainly very different from a hot-blooded Hungarian. He is reserved and controlled. He would never grab my hands in a public place or caress my knees under the table, which comes so easily to Hungarian men when they want to show their interest. He must know me better before he has the courage to hold me intimately.

I found him very interesting, maybe because of that difference. His foreign smile fired my imagination.

I wouldn't mind having him for a friend, I thought. He looks solid and stable as a rock.

As we sat by a window, we could see the castle of Eszterhazy standing in the distance on the other side of the park, and the statue of Haydn covered with snow. For a while we enjoyed watching the passersby hurrying and looking opaque through the icy windows.

"Everything looks black and white outside," Tom said. "I noticed that you think in colors while most people think in black and white like the scenery outside. I admire that about you. It makes you more interesting. The western world is very practical; practicality is the name of the game there."

"Miracles can only happen in the glorious adventures of a subjective mind," I said. "We Magyars are dreamers."

"Maybe it is the thousand-year-old past, the legends of the Kings who died for noble causes. Magyars are saturated with the legends of the past."

"How do you know?"

"From history books. I also know that throughout history you had a constant flow of invaders, the Germans, Austrians, the Tatars, the Turks…"

"The Soviets will stay forever," I sighed.

"I regret that we didn't help you when you asked for it. It was a mistake. Churchill predicted, when we were allies during the Second World War, that, if we allowed the Soviets to come to Europe, they would grab it and keep it in their iron grip. I am deeply sorry."

"The Hungarians will never hold that against your people. We are fascinated by Americans, and have always been fascinated by your country. Even when we were ordered to sing songs full of hatred against American Capitalists."

"I still feel ashamed," he said.

"I miss Budapest. It is a lovely place, beautifully situated like Rio, surrounded by blue mountains. The Danube flows through its middle. The Opera house is unique, even in Europe, with its Corinthian pillars, the elaborately carved statues of the muses on the roof, manicured parks, indoor and outdoor thermal baths, monuments dating back to the Romans."

"Tell me more about it. I always wanted to see Budapest, but it is too late now."

"Buda is my favorite place. Sometimes I stood still before a pastel-tinted villa, which past centuries left behind, gazing through the garden. I love Buda— The Royal Palace, the garden restaurants. I adore Budapest. I used to gaze at the cupola of the Cathedral, which is seen at it's best from the bridge. In pure air, every ornament in it could be clearly distinguished, glittering in the sunlight. Budapest is beautiful— it has a catch-in-the-throat quality. All that belongs now to the Soviet. Hungary is now a Russian satellite…"

He pitied me with his eyes. "Won't you have some tea now?" he asked. Twilight had fallen and a full moon was shining more and more brightly now outside, looking in at the windows. We sat there a long while, and the more silent the moonlight, the more violently my heart beat, till it was painful. It was a beautiful day, something to remember for a long time.

Chapter Four
LIFE IN THE BARRACKS

❦

SUMMER IS UTTER AGONY in the barracks. The rooms are beastly, hot day and hot night, regardless of how many times we try to create a draft by opening all the windows and the door. The big room I live in has only six windows, which is not enough since the room is divided by plywood walls into fifteen individual cubicles with three to four people living in each. Altogether about fifty-five souls live here dressed in human bodies with all the strange emanations of body and breath and unaired clothes. The room itself is dull, its basic color a neutral brown mixed with a sickly yellow, and dominated by the plywood walls. No matter how many times we crawl underneath the cots with a wet rag to clean out the dust, the room just stinks and stinks and stinks and the odor clings to our pores and to our hair no matter how frequently we wash ourselves in the shower room.

The barracks, called the Albrect Kaserne, is my home now. It is a military building converted into a refugee camp, approximately three thousand of us live supported by ten charitable organizations. The American Red Cross one of them. I moved here last year on a snowy afternoon, the day before New Year's Eve, and now it is already June. Six months have passed while I did nothing in particular—because I have nothing to do. I like to lie on my cot, which is the favorite pastime of everyone else in the big room with its plywood walls. People are lying on their cots reminiscing, while the sun rises higher and higher in the sky and the walls are drying up in the heat giving up crackling noises. Fortunately, we must get up three times a day in order to get in line in front of the mess wagons for our meals. Otherwise we would just lie on the cots stretched out and staring into space.

It is really surprising how fast the days go. Only the nights are unbearable because of the heat, which arrived bringing sticky days and hellish nights. It is almost impossible to sleep in the damp air of the room. So I follow the crowd as we go out to the yard carrying our blankets to lie down on the cement pavement along the stone walls that also radiate heat like an overheated oven. I try to get some sleep while the crickets, who live in swampy puddles on the neglected fields behind the barracks, are playing on their violins, and people are wandering around in nightgowns resembling ghosts searching for their forgotten past. Some of the young people make love in some corners and the shadows of the trees, taking advantage of the fact that the moon is hiding now behind dark, scattered clouds.

Outside the walls, Vienna is ready to greet the summer night, with doormen dressed like foreign generals standing by the revolving doors of the nightclubs. The evening sounds of the city and the smell of roasted duck, Wiener schnitzel and oysters emanates from the restaurants. When the night fragrance of the forest also comes in from the direction of the Kahlenberg, the night becomes seductive, irresistible and flamboyant, limousines and taxicabs circulating on the Ring with women bathed in strong perfume and men clad in tuxedo. In the gold-decorated show room German, Swedish and Morrocan girls are dancing under the rose-colored lights of the stage, their painted bodies glittering in the lights. The yard is in perfect stillness now. I gaze up into the sky where the moon is like a gleaming bridge of light swimming out slowly from behind the clouds. Memories come and nudge my elbow, leading me back to six months ago, the time when I arrived in Vienna in the red Citröen of the American reporter, Tom Allen. We had dinner together the day after he found out that all the refugees would be taken by train to the refugee camp in Tyroll. We sat in a nice little restaurant in Eisenstadt when he told me of his plan to "kidnap" me.

"I would hate to see you marching between armed guards from the schoolhouse to the railroad station," he said. "Besides… in Tyrol you would be buried in the camp for a long time because of the reorganization and red tape and all. You wouldn't be able to go to Vienna in a hurry and look for Tibor as I know you want to more than anything else. So I have decided I will take you there myself if you can manage to sneak out early in the morning. It is kind of selfish on my part because I would enjoy your company and wouldn't have to drive there alone since I must go there anyway on business."

I gladly accepted his offer. We arrived in Vienna in the early afternoon. After I recovered from the delightful shock of seeing the first big Western Metropolis of my life, I became alive with energy. The well-dressed people and shiny cars and well-stocked window displays were such a contrast with post-revolution Budapest, where the streets were soaked with blood, the buildings destroyed, and the people walked around in a daze. After having a cup of strong espresso coffee and a vanilla-scented brioche in a chocolate-smelling coffeehouse, I was eager to go with Tom to the Police station where we could locate Tibor's address.

To my surprise, he was living in the Palace of the Schwarzenberg's, at least that was the last address he filed with the police.

We drove to the Palace and Tom stopped the car in front of the wrought-iron fence. Through the car window we both looked at the magnificent Palace with admiration.

"What a place!" said Tom. "I suppose it is as luxurious inside as it is outside. I wonder how your friend got here? I wouldn't mind being the guest of the Schwarzenbergs for a while myself."

We got out of the car to say goodbye. He kept his fingers around my face and tightened his grip as he kissed my cheeks, holding me so close that I could see my miniature self in the iris of his eyes. He looked at me with a sadness, although he tried to conceal his emotions as if wearing a mask.

"Let me hear from you. Write me a postcard from New York when you get there and don't hesitate to call on me if you need anything in the future," said Tom as we parted. He remained standing by the fence as I left him and I went through the gate into the garden as in a dream. I could see a splendid garden, winter bushes and marble statues around a lake. The white marble statues of nymphs and satyrs stood looking at their own mirror images in the lake, which released a flow of images in me. There must be rooms in the Palace with Flemish portraits and marble archways, I thought, ballrooms with superfluous chandeliers and the faded smell of perfumed Dames who danced there a long time ago.

I'll see Tibor in a couple of minutes, I thought, and my heart contracted with fear thinking that he might not be in the Palace after all… that he might have moved somewhere else.

Something made me turn and look in the direction of the front gate. Tom was still standing there watching me, so I quickly waved a final farewell. He returned the wave, got into his car and drove away at a fast speed. I was surprised at the sadness I felt in seeing him leave. A friend was speeding away from me— a very good friend indeed, I thought, as I watched until his car vanished into the winterish afternoon. God knows if I will ever see him again, and I was again amazed at the ache in my heart— the same heart which pounded with joy a second before at the thought of meeting Tibor. I didn't have time to analyze the complexity of my feelings, however, my unexplainable mixture of feelings.

I rang the bell of the front door. A man came out dressed in livery and assured me that I was in the right place. "Yes. Mr. Erdes lives here in the Palace," he replied to my question. "Follow me, Ma'am," and he led the way. We climbed the curving backstairs and he left me in front of a chiseled door. I entered. I found myself in a dark room filled with dark, oblong and square furniture, a single ray of sun entering through a tall window where the draperies were drawn reflecting an rectangle of gold across an astoundingly green wall covered with faded silk.

There was an unset old wooden kitchen table in the front of a battered down, incredibly narrow sofa, a crystal vase on the top filled with dried Eucalyptus. Otherwise there wasn't a soul in the room, just me. I could hear the pounding of my heart.

Suddenly, he came out from somewhere and, seeing me, stood there speechless. Then he quickly came to me and took me in his arms.

It was a moment of immeasurable joy, the hysterical beating of my heart. I rested in his arms. Peace arrived in my existence with a sharp pain as if I was stabbed with a dagger. It was then I realized without a doubt that he was the only man I truly loved.

"This room belonged to the personal maid of the Princess. It is in the servants' quarters. You know, Darling, this isn't the way I dreamed I would receive you, but with flowers and with a four-wheeled carriage, the wheels studded with diamonds like in the fairy tales, rose petals your footsteps. I wanted to shower you with silver and gold, with all the flowers in the tropical gardens in the world."

I cried and I laughed at that silly talk. Then we kissed and kissed and kissed and later everything became simple.

I learned that I could not stay with him in the Palace since the Prince gave shelter only to male freedom fighters. There was no room in the Palace for women.

"I'll try to get you a room in a refugee camp, maybe the one at the Prater where I know the director," said Tibor. "The camps are very crowded at the present with refugees arriving each day by the hundreds." We took the streetcar to the outskirt of Vienna and after some negotiation with the jovial Austrian director of the camp; I was given a place in the barracks, a small cubicle in a large room with a cot, a table and a chair.

"Tomorrow will be New Year's Eve," said Tibor. "The first New Year's Eve we will spend together."

The next day he took me to a fashionable two-hundred-year-old restaurant where the walls were covered with autographed photos of famous people who once visited there, people with wealth and talent, movie stars and kings, the Prince of Wales among them and Edith Piaff and Mistinguette. I felt somewhat outlandish in my old and faded warm-up suit among the well-dressed people, but after an excellent meal of roast duck with orange sauce and a bottle of Tokai, I stopped caring about the way I looked. After we finished dinner I watched anxiously as the bill for our lavish meal arrived on a silver tray carried by a diplomatic-looking waiter clad in a kind of tuxedo.

"Don't worry, my love," said Tibor reading my thoughts. "I sold my grandfather's gold watch in an antique shop last night. That was the only valuable I brought with me, hidden in my shoes, when I bicycled across the border. Well, there was something else hidden in my shoes which I'll show you later," he added smiling secretively.

After midnight we joined the many people walking on the snowy streets and entering the different nightclubs where everyone was offered a free cup of hot tea laced with rum, and crispy ladyfingers in the tradition of Vienna on New Year's Eve. We kissed strangers wishing them *Fröhliche Weihnacht*[†]. Then around dawn we had coffee and brioche at a coffeehouse on the Ring.

Then right there before the very eyes of people who crowded the coffeehouse and the nice-looking waitress who brought the coffee, Tibor took out an old thin gold wedding ring from his pocket and he put it on my finger. "We are now

---
† Merry Christmas

engaged," he said with pride. "My Grandmother's old ring will bring us happiness and love forever!"

The waitress announced loudly to everyone in the room that there was an engagement here, and everyone cheered and wished us a happy life.

"Could we get married in the springtime, my love?" I asked him. "I always dreamed that the alter would be decorated on my wedding with lilies, you know the ones with long stems and strong perfume."

"You shall have it," said Tibor, "although I don't particularly like lilies. They remind me of death… like the candelabra and lilies at the sacrifice of Romeo and Juliet. But I will learn to like them if it makes you happy. You know I would bring the stars down from the sky for you!"

* * *

Six months have elapsed since that New Year's Eve and five months since Tibor was taken to a T.B. sanatorium somewhere near the Italian and Swiss border, called Bella Vista. It happened on a cold night in February when his fever rose so high that he became delirious and the ambulance came and took him away, screaming its way through the ice-covered streets. He got his cold working on the icy streets laying down cables for the Post Office. He had finally found the job at the beginning of January and it made him so happy because he could buy things for us that we needed badly. The streets of Vienna were covered with snow and ice all winter long and an icy wind blew each day he was working.

The doctor said both his lungs were affected by the cold. The doctor was so kind to us and didn't even charge money when we went to his office for the examinations. He knew as refugees we had no money or very little. He got a bed for Tibor in the sanatorium through the Quakers, an American organization that helped the refugees with everything from the day we arrived to Vienna. They also payed for all of Tibor's expenses, while in the sanatorium. The letters I received from Tibor were filled with optimism about his recovery. However, I also received a letter from his doctor indicating that things were not going so well. "His recovery is extremely slow. He is still contagious and feverish and has lost a lot of weight. We must consider the worst but there is always hope that he will get better because of his extremely strong will," he wrote. His doctor was not optimistic and I understood the message. I still hope that Tibor conquers the disease. I also know that the reason that his system is weak is because of the years he spent in the Communist jail. He barely survived on watery cabbage soup day after day after day, and stale bread. His system was deprived not only of proper nourishment but also fresh air, because the windows of his cell were covered with a thin piece of sheet metal to seal off the outside world.

    I am still hoping that one day Tibor will appear at the curtain of my niche, healthy and smiling. Until then I am waiting patiently. I have learned during the twenty-one short years of my life that waiting patiently pays off in the end. On occasion I do lose some of my patience, yet I am waiting all the same. I lie on my cot dreaming, mostly about our wedding that cannot be held in the springtime anymore. It is postponed indefinitely. But I am working on the details of our wedding with the magic brush of my mind, coloring everything with happy reds and mellow yellows and cobalt blues as if it were a painting by Brueghel. His pictures have such a wonderful effect on me. Whenever I get the chance, I go to the museum in the Burg. Occasionally when my mind gets tired of imagination and I need to do something else for recreation, I look out of the window of my cubicle. I consider myself very lucky to have a window. Most people's cubicles are along the walls with no windows. They must use flashlights whenever they want to read or write. Myself, I have an excellent view of the yard where the children play all day long in the dust, and after dark I can watch the lights coming from the big amusement park, the Prater… geometric red lights on the top of the trees playing carrousels, going round and round and round to the rhythm of the Riesen-Raad. I can also enjoy the smell of fresh-brewed coffee and the vanilla scent of the croissants, which comes from the nearby bakery every morning. I have learned that there are a lot of things in this life one can enjoy without having any money.

While Tibor was still here, we spent much of our time standing in line in front of the American Embassy trying to obtain a visa. (The lines were longer than the lines in front of the butcher shops back in Hungary.) Ninety-nine percent of the refugees want to emmigrate to the United States which is where Tibor and I dream of going. But our chances become very slight now that he has T.B. They don't accept people with lung diseases into the United States, I learned.

So I am very worried about our future and sometimes I forget my worries, all depending on the mood I am in… whether the sun shines or it rains… For a diversion and to kill time, I go to the warehouses of different charity organizations and I dig together with dozens of refugee women among tons of clothes sent to us by the free world on ships and planes.

Most of the clothes are from America. There are piles and piles of clothes, shirts and blouses, sweaters and all, piled up from floor to ceiling in the warehouses. A mixture of odors emanate from the clothes, the faint smell of powder and perfumes and individual skins pampered with showers and cold creams… There is the good smell of previous owners with bathrooms and with plenty of water to bathe in, the smell of a life style with no big worries, full stomachs and easy digestion. There is not a trace of the body odor in the clothes, which is so typical here in Europe, pungent and bitter and strong like the smell of an onion. I touch the cottons and silks and velvets with pleasure. For myself I find a basic black skirt and hand-knitted, violet-colored sweater that fits me perfectly. Then as I dig further, I find an evening gown made of white crepe de Chine. It is embroidered with white pearls. It has matching satin shoes tied around with a thin rope. (Why do they send us evening gowns? There is absolutely no chance for us to dance in ballrooms, except the feathery ball when we retire on our cots each evening.)

    I fell in love with the evening gown, although it was made for a bigger woman than me. I take it with me. It now hangs above my cot on a hanger. With a little imagination it could be a wedding gown. The pearls shimmer and shine in the evening lights. They reflect greens and blues and silvery soft pinks like the waves of the sea do under the summer sun.

    Ria comes into my cubicle almost every night for a good chat and she always has time before going to town to talk about the wedding I am planning when Tibor returns, including the way the gown should be altered to fit me a little better, taking in some seams and letting out some others.

Ria, the Hungarian gypsy girl with almond eyes and a voluptuous figure lives in a niche along the wall that has no window. She comes dressed for the evening, (she found some cocktail gowns at the warehouses), her thick curly hair piled up on her gracious head in the latest fashion. She has a lovely silk-textured, olive-colored skin and her eyes are as sleepy and mysterious as some of the exotic-looking queens of the Far East I used to see in the Spiegel. Our bare existence is quite disturbing here in the barracks where most of us don't have money to take the streetcar to the Graben, to splurge in the fashionable boutiques as Ria does. With her looks she creates a lot of excitement when she passes in the hallways in front of the men who gather there at all hours, and stare at her with lusty eyes. Even the married men talk about her with interest— in vain. She has boyfriends in the city, rich men with money and influence who shower her with gifts and money for her services. She usually leaves her four-year-old daughter, Micike, in my care. I tuck her in her bed when her mother leaves for the night. I tell her fairy tales until she closes her eyes, which are very similar to her mother's, velvety almonds.

The other day I caught Micike putting rouge on her face in front of the fly-speckled mirror in the shower room. Normally her face is very pale. Her skin has the color of dying roses because she never goes out to the yard to play with the other children. When I found her she looked made up like a little clown, the expression in her eyes mischievous and a little disturbing. She must have disappeared during the late afternoon while Ria was having her beauty sleep, her blanket pulled up to her nose, because when she woke up at supper time ready to dress and go out for the night, she couldn't find Micike. We looked for her in the shower room where she spends a lot of time lately bathing her porcelain doll in the bidet. She wasn't there. We couldn't find her anywhere. Around midnight, Ria lost control and began to cry and scream, telling everyone that her daughter probably got killed or something terrible happened to her. At twelve-thirty Micike arrived, brought in by the guard who had found her in a room that served as a storage room. He said he found her sitting behind an empty box in a daze. They took her to the doctor's office where her mother found out that she had been molested. She seemed not to have suffered any real psychological harm however. Micike was a tough little creature like her mother. She appeared to have survived the whole ordeal without a tremor.

"I can't be with you always," I heard Ria telling her after the commotion died down. "Next time (God forbid there *is* a next time) you will know how to scream and to kick and don't let any strangers get close to you!"

Ever since that incident, whether Ria is sleeping on her cot or goes downtown, I make sure I know Micike's whereabouts at all times. Sometimes we play army games, and I tell her over and over that she must learn how to defend herself to obey her mother and stay in the big room. Once in awhile, when Ria goes out during the day she takes me with her, usually when Walter, one of her steady friends, picks her up. On those occasions we leave Micike in the care of the Kleins, a nice couple who are my only neighbors in the cubicle next to mine.

Our favorite place in Vienna is the underground espresso of the opera house where we have coffee and croissants in the early afternoon. Walter stays for a while then leaves for his office and Ria and I stay to watch the tourists, mostly Americans, chatting enthusiastically in large groups. Sometimes we stay in the city after dusk and walk on the side streets near the opera house where we can see the prostitutes strolling around, sizing up the dollar-carrying American men… in vain. I have never seen any American leaving with any of the girls, they are too cautious. Mostly, it is the Italians and the Arabs who let themselves be lured by the girls into their small houses.

For some strange reason Ria loves to watch the prostitutes. I think she feels superior to them. She considers herself a high-class call girl, respectable in all aspects. Sometimes, one of her boyfriends Walter brings us American magazines where beautiful girls on the cover flash two rows of perfect teeth.

Walter often goes to New York on business trips. When he comes back he brings gifts to Ria, flashy-colored T-shirts and jeans. He returns with interesting stories about the lifestyle of the Americans.

"Over there it is very important to smile," he says. "People wear their smiles like banners. It is *essential*. If someone asks you how you are, you must say you are fine even if you're dying!"

* * *

Lying on the cot all day long and doing nothing is dangerous. One is inclined to fantasize and dream up absolutely non-existent things— for example… life without suffering. I like to fantasize about the lagoons of Venice, which I've never seen. Also, I think about the velvety coolness of the dark water at the Doge's Palace which stares at its own white marble reflection in the water. And when the bells of the Stefanskirche ring after dusk they make me think about my mother. I miss her terribly. I have always been an only child, loved to excess. We've been together since the day I was born. Now I worry about her safety back in Budapest. Each night I have a recurring dream. I am flying in the air with swimming motions, above sepia-brown fields and dark silent cities, heading toward Hungary. I search for my mother from house to house… in vain. The blood-red brick houses are empty and I know all the time, while searching for her, that she is dead. When I awake from those dreams I am drenched in perspiration. I haven't heard from her since I left Budapest.

* * *

The young, nice-looking black American man from the YMCA comes to the barracks teach us English twice a week. He stands at the pulpit like a black Othello, very debonair, unaware that the ladies in the class are enchanted by his looks. They look at him as though he were a big exotic bird flying here from the Pampas, strange and exciting, altogether different from the familiar European birds. They would like to catch the attention of his velvety dark eyes, while he talks about the fast-food business, the soft drinks in America and gives statistics on the number of yellow school buses all over in the American suburbs.

"In America each person owns a bed," he says, and I wonder why he tells us that. Does he think that in Communist Hungary we all slept on the floor? I, too, share the ladies' interest in our teacher. I understand their curiosity because in Budapest there was only one black man who we knew came there after the war and who worked as a waiter in a fashionable espresso in Buda. He used to carry his trays of coffee with tango steps, light and alien, and we loved him and spoiled him with large tips which he took with a gentle smile on his ebony face.

Our black teacher gives us a friendly advertisement about the fast food business, about the hot dog and hamburger stands unknown to us in Europe. He arouses our curiosity about his faraway land. I manage to buy a bottle of Coca-Cola at a nearby espresso coffee house, one of the few that has soda machines in Vienna. It tastes like medicine.

* * *

Our life in the barracks is a strange combination of excitement and absolute despair. Visas are hard to obtain, especially American visas. Too many undesirable elements came to Vienna with the first wave of refugees, members of the Communist Party, Secret Policemen who had tortured people, and common criminals who fled when the freedom fighters opened the doors of the jail. Members of the secret police and common criminals were the first ones to get to Vienna and that is the reason the Americans are more cautious in issuing visas. Now they are taking their time.

The worst thing is that Tibor is not here. I miss him terribly. I am worried about his health. During the day I am all right, but the nights bring despair. I cry a lot through the cover of the night.

I am utterly lonely. The only friends I have are Ria, the Kelemens, and Maca. The Kelemens are a couple in their thirties who live in the cubicle on one side of me. Steven Kelemen is a newspaperman from Budapest, a hunchback with an impressive head on his small, fragile body. He has larger-than-life eyes with a hint of melancholy in them. He spends a lot of time rearranging his books, which he keeps in cardboard boxes under the cot. He carried those books with him in a knapsack across the border. He has Plato and Cassius, Dickens and Proust, Puskin and Balzac, and others. He is deeply in love with his wife, Melitta, who is a tall statuesque blonde built like the Venus de Milo. They have a two-year-old girl named Lillian who is in a nursery school up on the Kahlenberg, along with many of the children recovering from the shock of their escape, when they walked through frightening forests and icy brooks in order to get to the land of Freedom.

Lillian, like so many babies during the exodus, had to be given some barbiturates so as not to be discovered by the guards patrolling the area while her parents waded through the swamps to get to Austria. They had no other choice when she began to cry from exhaustion and hunger and fear. The trees in the forest only magnified her cries in the silence of the night. They were forced to administer the drug.

Lillian looks healthy and wonderful now, but she has a heart murmur that the doctor discovered during a routine physical examination. This was not uncommon among refugee children who had to go through the same ordeal.

Steve and Melitta are in love. They make love frequently; their moans can be heard through the walls of the cubicle during the night. Their love is the only solid thing they have. They often invite me for a gourmet meal that Steve cooks over the Sterno burners, like potato *paprikash* with slivers of sizzling bacon. He cooks and he sews dresses by hand from materials he gets from the warehouses. He brushes Melitta's long blonde hair until it flutters like the wings of a butterfly. After dinner we sit cross-legged on the cot, the air filled with the smell of burned lard. Steven is citing a passage from Le Saule, "*Le phalène doré, dans sa course légère, Traverse les prés embaumés.*" The smell of food and the noise of the crowded room are overwhelming. The words of Rimbaud are light and transparent as the Brussels lace on my grandmother's wedding gown.

Chapter Fourteen
THE AMERICAN REPORTER

TOM ALLEN MUST HAVE WRITTEN the postcard a few days before his flight because according to the calendar he would arrive the day after I received his card. Unconsciously or with intention, he was giving me to a fait accompli thereby removing the necessity of having to decide whether I wanted to see him or not. He left me no choice. I had written to him occasionally and so he knows that Tibor is in the Bella Vista but aside from that he knows nothing about my personal life— about the crazy days in the barracks and about my lonely days and nights. He has no idea how I am longing to meet an old friend like him to ease the burden of my loneliness. The day he was to arrive I dressed with great care. I waited for him at the gates impatiently, the hours going by slowly until I saw his taxicab arrive. My heart contracted as he stepped out from the cab. I realized I was more than happy to see his gleaming American smile showing thirty-two healthy white teeth. He looked at me in such a way that I knew he was happy to see me too.

He must notice that I am not my old self anymore, I thought. He must surely notice that. I smiled at him revealing my heart and also my tears that came unexpectedly.

"Forgive me," I said. "But I am really touched that you came."

"I had to," he answered. "It has been so long. I've thought about you a lot."

"Can we go to dinner somewhere?" I asked him. "But I must get back before midnight. They close the gate of the barracks at midnight."

"How about going to Grinzing?"

"I could never resist a man inviting me to one of those charming garden restaurants. "I said jokingly, drying my nose and tears with his handkerchief."

"I have already finished with business, I am all yours," he said. "I am at your service, my mysterious pale Princess."

The afternoon was blue and gold and perfumed from summer beneath a cloudless sky in Grinzing. The air was warm and light as an electric blanket. The garden restaurant was filled with people eating and drinking and singing, the trees like huge tents made out of dense foliage hanging above the tables, the flowerbeds by the stone wall filled with flowers of all kind, white and pink and red heads pushing themselves aggressively above the white gravel as if to get a better view.

The smell of *wiener schnitzel*† served with crispy brown deep fries and the aroma of white wine made me feel dizzy. Or was it the golden eyes of the reporter looking at me with such manifest happiness. I wasn't sure.

† a traditional Austrian dish

"Your appetite is the same," he said. "I could never tire of watching you eat."

"Can I order *Gundel palacsinta*‡?" I asked him. "I saw it on the menu. You should try it yourself. It is a poem made of thin pancakes with layers of nuts and rum and chocolate sauce."

"New York was gray and wet and the air full of carbon monoxide as I boarded the plane," he said. "I forgot how nice Vienna could be in summertime— vibrant and lively like you."

"C'mon, don't flatter me," I said. "Don't take advantage of the fact that I love to be flattered!"

"You've got it," he replied. "Anything you want. How about another portion of Gundel palacsinta?"

After dinner we took a long walk on the pastel-colored streets alongside the small, yellow-painted houses as the stars in the sky were just coming out to celebrate the glory of the night.

For a while we sat on a bench and watched a young girl dressed in a flowered skirt and a white lace blouse dancing by herself to the *schrammelmusik*§ coming from the gardens, her blonde hair bouncing to the rhythm of the crying guitars. Her friend, an equally blonde young Frenchman, sitting on a low stone wall followed her with his eyes. Content couples strolled on the streets coming out from restaurants filled with music and the smell of beer. Rounded women with creamy complexions accompanied their men, all of them happy and tipsy, and alive with laughter.

"It looks like a scene from an operetta," I said.

---

‡ crêpe-like variety of Hungarian pancake
§ a style of Viennese folk music

"I would give anything to chase away the clouds from your eyes," he said.

"It's a happy night," I said, "I am only just a little moody when the sky is like black velvet and the stars like small camp fires burning. It has the same effect on me, always. I feel that deep hunger in me, sweet and sad and unexplainable."

"I know the feeling, it comes when I am watching the sunset in a strange city. It comes suddenly, the feeling of sadness."

"I am glad that you understand. The feeling is similar to what one feels when the föhn blows in Vienna ruffling the magnolia trees with electric madness."

"Should we go up to the Kahlenberg tomorrow— a picnic on the grass? Or should we explore Schönbrunn, the golden rooms of the Kings and Emperors?"

"Kahlenberg would be fine, a picnic on the grass…" I said.

"Fine. I love picnics. We Americans are famous for having picnics. The woods in America are filled with the charcoal smell of hamburgers, all over… I'll pick you up early in the morning."

Next morning he arrived with a bag of food, jars of caviar, cheese and fresh Viennese bread. We took the cable car up to the mountains and had a feast under an old tree then gathered wild flowers. About dinnertime we found a rustic restaurant where he ordered cappuccinos. Drinking them, we watched the sunset from the small balcony, the roofs and windows of Vienna burning below from its rays.

He waited until the last rays of sunset sank beneath the horizon and the world wrapped itself in darkness. Then he touched my hand with his hands.

"I love you!" he said. "I have, from the beginning…"

"It is the night of true confessions," I said, and I didn't have the strength or desire to withdraw my hands... It felt like arriving in a warm room after being in the cold for a long time.

"I must confess that I have feelings for you too, you are so kind, very romantic for an American..."

"My head is spinning from your closeness," he said. "And never mind what you've heard about Americans."

I felt him trembling as I kissed him.

"It comes from the bottom of my heart," I said. "Thank you for everything, for the money you sent to Switzerland for the doctor..."

"I did it for you," he said. "I am a funny guy. I was asking for the best treatment for your love, Tibor. It is nonsense..."

The next day we went out to the airport together. There was still an hour until his plane was to depart so we drank hot chocolate in the small airport restaurant. It was full of people waiting for someone or saying goodbye to someone while others just sat at the tables staring ahead.

"How sad that someone is always saying goodbye," I said to Tom. "Someone is always coming into our lives or leaving. We only meet for what seems like a brief moment."

"Like two ships passing at sea," he said.

He made me promise that I'll write to him.

"I will always be there for you," he told me.

I watched his plane getting smaller and smaller on the cobalt-blue sky, looking like a silver-winged seagull. Then I went back to the restaurant and ordered myself a plum-schnapps (Tom had given me some spending money before he left). Afterwards, all my emotions rose to the surface and I cried the entire way home, not really knowing why.

* * *

Two letters were waiting for me in the mailroom, one from Tibor and the other one from mother. Her letter was cheerful and full of humor despite the fact that she had been evicted from the house right after the secret police discovered that I had left for Austria. Her furniture was thrown all over the muddy street. She makes funny remarks about the small room she was given at the hospital, a room at the end of the lobby, close to the toilet, from where the asthmatic leaking of the faucet can be heard all night long, as well as the palavering of the patients who gather in the lobby for an evening chat.

Tibor's letter is happy. He is expressing hope that he'll soon come home, and we can then proceed with our wedding plans.

I read both letters over and over until I know the words by heart. "The clean air and sunshine are doing wonders," writes Tibor. "In case you happen to call Dr. Ehren, don't believe what he says. I just know that I'll see you soon. I love you more than words can say."

I gain my strength from the letters; they lift my spirits. The sun must shine all over the globe, (although Vienna has been soaked in rain for the last couple of days, in never ending rain) and the card I receive from Tom Allen also proves it.

"I am in Miami attending a conference, getting high on sunshine. My next business trip will be to Vienna. I don't know the exact date yet. I'm looking forward to spending a few days with the Hungarian princess. Adieu, *mon plaisir*[¶]; may we meet again."

I keep the letters underneath my pillow neatly folded in a handkerchief. I feel the written words all over my body, even when I sleep…

* * *

The Kelemen's, Ria and Maca are my only friends. With the Kelemen's we understand each other. They are wonderful people. We often go out together, (only when they have some extra money to spend) to that cheap little fast food place on the Ring. Here they buy me a big portion of crispy fried fish and some beer. Here we are, in that clean, small place, inhaling the smell of fish, jabbering away as if we had known each other for years. We exchange jokes with the plump, blonde Austrian waitress.

I have the same warm, trusting relationship with Ria. We love to stroll together on the narrow streets of the old district of Vienna, that is, when she is not dating. We wander around enjoying the shimmering lights on the Danube. Sometimes we sit on the marble bench by a leaping, cold fountain. Always talking of men and love. Ria is warm, funny, and very egocentric. She has that *"L'état c'est moi"*

[¶] my pleasure

attitude. She is a little vulgar at times, but she never pretends to be something she is not, and that is why I like her.

With Maca, it is very, very different. She follows me around since the first day we met; (in the dark, long, gray lobby) she follows me constantly. I found it difficult to get away from her demand of attention. She tells me this, she tells me that, she sells me lurid stories of the belly dancers in the barracks, of the white slavery traffic. She loves to talk about her life back in Budapest. She tells that she always had plenty of money. Even during the darkest days of socialist economy. She had enough money to buy everything she ever wanted, even more, she tells me. She behaves like a deposed Queen. There is a Wagnerian atmosphere about her, very smug.

Why did she escape? Why did she leave Hungary when she had such a good life there? She is like a murky river, I can't see through her. When I see that lemon colored shrewdness in her eyes I decide not to trust her. But invariably I give her a chance, because I am lonely and I need to talk to someone.

Chapter Sixteen
MACA

I MEET WITH MACA IN THE SHOWER room every day when everyone else is gone so we can hedonize with a long leisurely shower and sit on the bidet for a long time. Meanwhile Maca talks and talks and talks and has no interest whatever in what I have to say. She lives across the lobby in another big room divided with plywood walls, even more crowded than ours and more stinky. She never visits anybody, being something of a snob and inclined to look down on anyone with less education than hers. She speaks fluent German and French and Yiddish and was educated in the Sacré Coeur convent school. She holds her forty-five-year-old head proudly on her skinny body, as though she were a star in Hollywood. She thinks the people in the barracks are proletarians, with a few exceptions. I must fit the measure of her expectations for some reason or other, because she seems to favor my companionship.

"You finished at Sacré Coeur," she says. "You are a lady, *n'est ce pas?*† You look clean, clean and well groomed. People here act like pigs. They make a mess of themselves and their cots."

So we sit on the bidet while other people take naps in their cubicles. The shower room is in heavenly stillness, only the splashing of water can be heard and Maca's thin little voice so much in contrast to her middle-aged looks.

She massages herself with cold cream all over, while she gazes at me with a critical stare as if measuring me up.

"You have looks similar to Marlene Dietrich," she says, "hollow cheeks and eyes far apart. That is the look most men are attracted to."

She studies me as though I were a racehorse or a new call girl in the local bordello.

"The only thing which needs more attention is your skin," she continues.

"You should take care of your skin and use expensive creams. I am forty-five years old but I don't have any wrinkles. I have never been married and that could help also. My dear old mother warned me that people usually get wrinkles from making love, although she had eight children and her face was rosy and flawless like that of a china doll's. My poor mother had a lot of children and a lot of money but no happiness at all. Don't ask me why. She was just the kind of person who is never happy no matter what. We traveled a lot, spending the summers in Abbazia and Rimini as far back as I can remember. We were always rich, before and after and during the war. Father had an umbrella business. People needed umbrellas; rain always falls from the sky. We had villas and maids and chauffeurs and all the luxuries…

---

† isn't it so?

except one… a bathroom with good plumbing. Remember the struggles to stoke up the boilers to provide hot water? I have an Uncle in Brooklyn who I'm told has the most luxurious bathroom imaginable," she said, with little tremors of desire in her voice. She opened a small tube and smeared its pink contents all over herself. "I have something on my mind," said Maca. "I have a friend, a Hungarian businessman who travels all over the world. He needs someone to type for him. He would pay good money. I thought about you. You could make money and buy things, silk stockings, creams and Coty perfumes. You should really do more than lie on your cot all day."

* * *

"America is the richest country in the world," says Maca. We are in the shower room again, enjoying the hot splashes of the bidet, one of our favorite pastimes. We can't seem to get enough water to wash ourselves all over, top and bottom, in an effort to get rid of the stale smell of the pillows and sheets on the cots. The smell seems to stick to our bodies permanently like a layer of skin.

Maca loves to talk about bathrooms and cold creams, which are her favorite topics. "My dream is to live with my uncle in Brooklyn. I hope to get the visa soon," she tells me. "Americans have the most perfect plumbing in the world, showers and bathtubs, constantly available hot water in the bathrooms, hygienic tile floors, etc., etc. They have everything, good food and plenty of it. American society enjoys the distinction of being the most progressive society in the world. Now tell me, what do you want to do with your life? Here in the barracks you are only a small fish among the thousands of fishes struggling for air, washed ashore. You should seriously consider my offer. My friend, the traveling businessman is returning in about two weeks. He sent me a postcard. He is anxious to get help, light typing. I have the key to the doctor's office; don't ask me how I was able to get it. You can practice there during the nights. If you aren't interested in buying something for yourself, consider how nice it would be to have enough money to visit Tibor in the Bella Vista!"

(She seems to know everything about my life.)

"Now you're more convincing. You know I would do anything to be with Tibor," I say. "I would walk into the lion's cage to see him. You just talked me into it. When can you give me the key to the doctor's office?"

"Great! I can give you the key right now. I keep it under the mattress."

"I've never cared for creams and perfumes. I don't type well. My education was in the Classics, I can quote poems in German and French, I can quote Cicero… *Quo usque tandem abutere Catilina, patientia nostra…* But I can't type."

"You are a lady, among other things," she said.

"Not always. I made a big scene the other day in the shower room, I scratched Mrs. Baja's arm with my fingernails, because she called my friend, Ria, a prostitute. I scratched her so badly that she was bleeding."

"But that is exactly what I mean, you've got guts, and all," she said.

After that discussion I didn't see her for a long time. I felt sick, I had to go to the doctor in order to ask him to do something about the uneasy feeling in my stomach. It had been in my stomach for a long time. I felt tired and irritable.

"Take two blue pills after each meal, and the pink barbiturates before you go to sleep," said the doctor, giving me the same faded smile he gave in turn to everyone sitting on the benches. He was in a hurry; he had to attend a party in Grinzing with his wife. He gave orders to his assistant, a blonde woman with an indifferent air, to stab me with a needle.

"You will feel brand new," she said.

She doesn't have any idea that pills have never helped me. Nor have injections. She lives in a plastic house where the windows are green from the view of the garden. She is surrounded with pink mountains of laughter of her chubby children who bring her happiness. She has a well-organized and secure life.

How could she understand my problems?

She puts some pink and blue pills in a small paper bag, counting them carefully. Maybe it is my doomed past or my uncertain future but, in spite of the barbiturates, I still cannot sleep. I turn my eyes toward the dark ceiling counting Hungarian poodles but I still don't drift off to sleep. Meanwhile, the air gets stuffy from the breathing of those who are already sleeping.

I'm bothered by my thoughts. There is an acne-faced young man who has been paying a lot of attention to me. He has shiny black hair and he seems to be everywhere. For all I know he may be a disguised AVH man sent here by the Hungarian government. Everyone knows that there are AVH men living among us in the barracks, under the same roof, spying on our moods and political activities. They are watching us like vultures and eavesdropping on our conversations. And they are as slippery as fish. The Cafes and popular restaurants are full of them. They sit hiding behind magazines like in spy movies. They try to get you into conversation. The presence of the agent provocateurs proves that the arms of the Hungarian secret police are long— they reach everywhere. (Budapest is only an arm-length distance from Vienna.)

Last night the dark-haired AVH man haunted me again in my dreams, probably because of his ubiquitous presence yesterday. He had followed me all over. He showed up at the underground Espresso where I went window-shopping. I stood in front of a magazine stand looking for the new edition of Spiegel, looked up and saw his smiling face right before me. His smile was like that of a merchant who wants to sell you his leftover goods, the ones that smell of rotten eggs, all the time trying to convince you of their freshness. "How are you?" he asks. "I've seen you around in the barracks. You are so pretty, and you are not a snob at all! How about a cup of coffee?"

"No thank you, I had my espresso already, but thanks anyway," I said trying to escape… He persisted. "Let me buy you a slice of *Sachertorte*‡ and a glass of milk— my favorite combination."

"Not mine, thank you. I am on my way home." I turned to go but he grabbed my hand. "Too bad! We could have such a good time. I admire you. I envied the man I used to see you with, you know that tall, auburn-haired guy, dressed like an American. Is he really an American? He had that flair about him, tall and well dressed and all."

---

‡ chocolate gateau with apricot jam filling and chocolate icing

"He is the head of a well-known spy ring. I sold him top secrets. He paid me well. I am loaded with the green dollar," I told him.

He looked at me with the face of a cupid, smooth and innocent and naive. "I love your excellent sense of humor. You are gamine, like a Parisian. Please don't turn down my next offer. I'd like to invite you to see "Gone With The Wind." It's playing in that cozy cinema at the end of the Ring somewhere. I'll get a taxi."

"I don't understand. Why this sudden interest in me?"

"Because you are the most intelligent girl in the barracks— beautiful, smart, and sophisticated! I was hoping to have a stimulating conversation with you. Sorry, if you think I was coming on too strong."

"Guten Tag [§]*,"* I replied. "Please stay away from me in the future…"

"Very well, Fräulein, *entschuldige bitte*[¶]," he said, changing the conversation to German. Then he left like a matador, the one who just destroyed the bull. Back in the Barracks, I couldn't eat my supper, noodles topped with cabbage, which was my favorite. The smile of the disguised AVH man made me sick. I couldn't get his slimy smile out of my mind.

* * *

[§] good day!
[¶] please excuse me

Authorities have warned us that money supplied by different charity organizations is running out, and refugee camps all over Austria are having financial difficulties. The number of refugees has now grown to an incredible two hundred thousand, and people are still arriving. They are still crossing the Austrian-Hungarian border under terrible circumstances, many times shot at and wounded, and always harassed by the Communist frontier guards.

Our life in the barracks hangs on a thread. It hangs on a thread economically and morally. We are worried and we are frightened, because we detect impatience in the attitude of the Austrian staff.

"Get the hell out of here," their eyes seem to be saying. "We are getting tired of serving you."

I might be imagining all this, or I might not. The doctor and the chef in the kitchen and the director of the camp are still doing their best to help us. They are busy helping us. Yet I start to feel like a pariah, as if I had leprosy. Like for example today: we had some American visitors, just at the moment we started to line up in front of the food-wagons. We were in the lobby, holding our plates, inhaling the stench of the toilets, which was stronger than ever, mixed with the smell of the cabbage. The Americans had come to inspect the conditions of the barracks, we were told. Their group consisted of three cotton-haired ladies and two husky men wearing baggy pants and big, awkward shoes. I looked at them and I felt unwashed and unkempt, while they looked extremely healthy, well fed and rosy-cheeked. And also sterilized.

They watched us with friendly smiles and with a kind of perverse curiosity. I got my soup and then I retreated as fast as I could, retiring to my cage. I sat on my cot, the bowl of soup on my lap, tears of humiliation in my eyes.

* * *

"I have a date with Miklos, that debonair Hungarian," said Ria. "I don't usually accept dates with my compatriots, for various reasons, but this guy has money and connections. He invited me to the opening of a new coffee house in town. He wants me to bring another girl. I thought about you."

"Who is he?"

"He is a friend of a friend. I have a suspicion that he is a big shot somewhere. I don't know where."

"Something doesn't sound right, Ria. How can a refugee have money? The Austrian authorities don't even allow us to find work."

"I don't really care who he is. I just care that he is loaded!" she replied.

"Now be a good sport and come along, O.K.?"

"How shall we dress?"

"In your best. I'll lend you my ice-blue lace blouse."

There was a colorful crowd at the coffee house when we arrived there; the cream of Vienna Society was there. It was a nice place with contemporary, beige-colored tables and chairs, live trees and bushes planted in big stone urns, which exhaled their sweet smell of oxygen. Tropical birds sang in wicker cages hanging from ropes above the tables, they swung from the breeze every time someone opened the door. The blue light of the Viennese afternoon looked in through the windows, staring at the milky- skinned housewives and their spouses, elegant film divas and high-class call girls, as well as officers from the Army. Everyone was stuffing themselves with petits fours filled with chocolate and cream and rum and drank innumerable liqueur glasses of Cointreau.

Our Hungarian dates waved to us from a table. They were well dressed in conservative black suits and introduced themselves as Miklos and Pali. Miklos was tall with brown eyes and olive skin, while Pali was a skinny blonde. They both wore shiny black patent-leather shoes. They looked well groomed and were perfumed like some gigolos, and had smooth manners. They greeted us by kissing our hands, as was the custom, and they ordered us each a schnapps.

We sat for a few hours inhaling the smoke of American cigarettes that the whole crowd seemed to be smoking. Then Miklos invited us to his apartment.

"I would like to present you with something nice," he said. "I have fur coats and beautiful leather shoes from the American Red Cross and from other charity organizations. You can choose whatever you want, before I distribute it to the other refugees. Fine things for two fine ladies, you two come first."

"Thank you," I said. "But I don't think we should go."

"Let's go and see your place," said Ria.

"Don't be a chicken, they'll not bite!" she whispered to me teasingly.

We took a taxicab and arrived at a big apartment complex where Miklos lived on the third floor. His room was simple and well heated, with yellow furniture in good taste. There were dozens of paper boxes all over the place, covering the bed, the chairs and the floor. Some beautiful fur coats lay on the divan spread out like dead animals. Ria was thrilled and right away she tried on a few, finally selecting a beige-colored mink.

"Try on the white lamb!" she urged me, and when I did, she praised both me and the coat. "You look like Michelle Morgan in that coat!" she exclaimed.

"We cannot possibly accept these. They must be terribly expensive," I said to the two men.

"Please accept them. Just remember that I didn't buy them, they were the gift of the free world. And you will give me great pleasure in accepting them!"

I marveled at the brand-new patent-leather shoes all around the bed and underneath.

"They aren't mine," replied Miklos. "They're part of a shipment from other countries across the ocean. They too will be distributed. I only took one pair for myself."

"You must have good connections among the authorities of warehouses," Ria said to Miklos.

"I do," he answered. "Very good connections."

The two Hungarians behaved like gentlemen, yet under the surface they seemed more like con artists. We talked and they served us some wine.

Miklos invited us the following day to go to a Hungarian restaurant to have *chicken paprikas***.

At around midnight, we thanked them for everything and left, taking the streetcar back to the barrack.

"Do you want to meet them again? Are you thinking of continuing the friendship with Miklos?" I asked Ria.

"Absolutely not!" she replied. "I got what I wanted. I have a feeling that I shouldn't see him anymore. Don't ask me why— I just feel it. I have a beautiful coat and so do you! It isn't so bad having a friend like me, is it?"

**   a popular Hungarian dish

Even if she had wanted to see Miklos again, it wouldn't have been possible because he disappeared from the scene as quickly as if he had never been here. We heard later that he was an important person sent to Vienna by the Hungarian communist government. He was carrying secret information imbedded in the sole of his shiny black-patent leather shoes. We learned that he went back to Budapest and was given an important job in the government.

"He was a 'con artist' after all," said Ria. "But in a different sense from me. He was a traitor, a phony. All the talk about connections and all and how much he could help the refugees!"

Meanwhile, Ria paraded all over Vienna showing off her new fur coat. I couldn't wear mine. I was ashamed.

"You are a fool for not enjoying that lovely coat!" she said to me. "You should learn how to pick cherries when there are no cherries on the table of your life. Everybody creates his own luck."

"I don't quite agree with your philosophy," I told her. "Yet I must admit that in some respects you are right. The question is what will happen to our immortal souls if we deny our conscience and accept expensive things in return for nothing?"

"You're wrong," she said. "You should thank God that you didn't have to sell yourself for it. Some people do. You didn't have to go to bed with the man and you still got the coat, didn't you?"

"How lucky can I get?" I said sarcastically. Then I offered her a pack of Lucky Strike, the last one I had and had been saving. She had been looking at it with such desire in her eyes (it had been on top of my cot) that I had to offer it, although she didn't ask for it and I knew she had packs of

American cigarettes in cartons under her cot. After all she was my friend and because of her I gained a nice fur coat and perhaps some good advice after all.

* * *

Suddenly, I am so sought after by old and newly found friends, that I don't have time to lie on my cot and daydream, or to stroll on the streets watching the shadows and lights, or be getting high on the scents and sounds of Vienna, as amusing and refined as an international courtesan dressed in silk and velvet and bathed in the perfume of music.

I spend the nights in the doctor's office where I practice typing by the light of the street lamp coming through the windows, afraid to turn on the ceiling light because I am using the room illegally.

Each afternoon I am invited to the social room by Juci, a newly acquired friend whom I met a few weeks ago when she arrived at the barracks with her ex-husband. For some reason or other, they escaped together and made their way through icy rivers and dark forests from Budapest to Austria, helping one another in every possible way.

They have held hands and behaved like lovers since the day they checked in, giving the impression that they are considering patching up the broken mosaic of their marriage. But that impression is deceptive because while she is working on her future career of becoming a showgirl, he is hypnotizing the ladies of the barracks and luring them to his bed with his penetrating blue eyes. He also has the talent of telling their fortunes from their palms and from the configuration of the stars, which he studies industriously from big astrology books piled upon each other by his cot.

He says, "By profession I am an electrical engineer but my hobby is calculating the effect of the stars on people's lives." His cubicle is usually crowded with ladies of all shapes and hair colors who hang on his lips as he embroiders tales about the influence of the capricious stars on their lives.

Juci is statuesque and extremely feminine, with her peaches-and-cream aura that emanates from her like the faded fragrance of youth. She behaves like a teenager with a slight air of hysteria, while in fact she is already pushing thirty.

All this is very becoming to her, the male population of the barracks whistles in admiration as she passes them on the way to the social room, her high-heeled shoes click-clacking on the gray stone floor of the lobbies. She is always in a hurry, giving the impression that she flies over the disinfectant-smelling lobbies rather than walks, giving off flame-colored energy sparks in contrast to her pale femininity.

"You should join us," she says to me as I watch the dancing. The good-looking girls with shapely bodies are preparing themselves to be part of a show in Tangier and Yemen and Morocco to which they will be transported in the near future following their training. While I watch them, I hear stories about the dark-skinned Arabs who favor fair-skinned European girls and I hear about the fortunes some of the girls have already made in the Far East— jewelry and diamonds and all.

The girls are swirling and bending, shaking their bellies; the room is filled with the musty odor of their young bodies. Juci is dancing in the front line, her hair burning in the afternoon sun like a flame-colored torch. There is a sweet-sounding oriental melody on the tape, the sound of tambourines, harps, flutes and pipes, which encircles the room like the thin smoke of opium. Through the open window the smell of burning myrrh drifts in from the chapel at the opposite side of the yard. Their people are gathering for the Litany, the brown benches crowded with refugees begging God to hasten their visas and passports.

The turgid music of the East mingles with the holy songs and it sounds as though two stations were being heard simultaneously on the radio.

To kill time I watch the girls. In the misty rays of late sunset they look like the women of a harem in some jaded fantasy of the East, fragile and fluid, with dark circles under their eyes.

The middle-aged woman making costumes on the old Singer sewing machine talks to me in a singsong voice and tries to persuade me to join the group. Her eyes are accented with kohl and cobalt blue, giving her the look of a "Madam" in a high-class whorehouse. Meanwhile she tries hard to behave like a *gnädige Frau*††… picking up the shimmery materials from the floor all round her fastidiously as if she had no connection with these flimsy suggestive dresses.

She and a fat agent arrived from the city a few weeks ago, as uninvited and unexpected as death, acting like Papa and Mamma, taking care of their lost children. The fat agent jokingly refers to the barracks as the "lost paradise."

He sits on a rickety chair, his octopus eyes and his sallow complexion, as starchy as potato pie. But he is a good agent. The girls drink in his promises like nectar as he talks of the glamour of their future lives in the Far East, and

---

†† madam

blows acrid smoke from his cigar through his lumpy nose with its enlarged pores. They laugh at his jokes revealing his bad teeth… To me he looks rather like a salesman from hell instead of the good Godfather the girls believe he is. But who am I to judge?

The tape is still playing as I leave the room to be on time for supper in front of the mess wagon. Then my routine continues. I go to the doctor's office to practice typing. Around dawn I have a Lucullus feast with Maca in her cubicle as we gorge ourselves on *pâté de foie gras* (which she buys with the green dollars her uncle sends her from Brooklyn) smeared generously on the stale black bread she saved from lunch.

I have a few hours of sleep, tossing and turning and woken by the street noises, until finally Juci arrives with a pot of weak coffee that she brings me each morning as a token of her friendship.

While I sip the coffee she describes again the joy of being a showgirl in the Far Fast, her freckles soft and golden like miniature daisies on her cheeks.

* * *

"You look as if all the faded grays and greens of the barrack walls were smeared on your face! You need diversion. So you're invited tonight to the corner restaurant to have a drink with me while I wait for Kurt," says Ria… So I go. I have been accepting every invitation I receive and am becoming a social butterfly lately.

Later, as I sit in the rectangular room of the restaurant, which is dark and filled with the smell of spilled beer and wine, I almost wish I hadn't come. I realize I am becoming paranoid, feeling nauseous whenever some stranger looks into my face on the streets. Right now I feel like a washed-out rag, like the one the bartender is using to clean the sticky glasses. I wonder why I feel that way; my stomach contracts and I perspire from some unknown fear. The fine hair on my arms and elsewhere stands erect from some sinister feelings— real or imaginary.

Just at this moment a group of young local "studs" arrive, letting in the outside breeze. They are loud and unpredictable, dressed in elegant-looking rags, and having long noses, and triangular eyes in Lombroso-type faces. They startle me and I spill the Bénédictine that the funny-looking bartender served me in a tiny glass.

"What *is* the matter, Kinga? You look like a rabbit frightened by a spotlight," says Ria trying to keep me from jumping off the barstool. If I could analyze the deterioration of my spirit, I would say that since the Revolution I have been frightened by certain kinds of situations and places and people. And my symptoms have become worse since I began this typing job for that strange man. Maca's so-called "friend" about whom I know nothing.

A fear is growing inside me as if it were a cancerous growth— a kind of precognition— cruel and inexplicable. Whenever I ask Maca to tell me about him, she is evasive either because she doesn't know or she's hiding something.

"He will be generous with money." That is all she says in answer to my inquiries.

The day when he will return from the business trip in Rimini hangs over my head like the sword of Damocles.

Yet I have made up my mind to finish the business I started. I am not going to retreat. It isn't my personal style to retreat anyway.

     So I type and type and type until one day Maca comes to my cubicle, breathless as if she had just won a Marathon race and tells me that her "friend" is coming back. He wants me to go to his hotel for an interview the following day. I choose the dress I will wear very carefully and decide on a black pleated skirt and a high-necked white blouse to look ladylike and businesslike. I tried to avoid anything provocative since I have never been in a hotel room with a strange man before.

     The hotel he lives in is in a seedy district of Vienna. It is a non-significant building on a non-significant street. Street urchins are playing in front of its peeling walls when I arrive. Women dressed in printed frocks hurry by with huge wicker baskets stuffed with potatoes and onions and the entire street smells like a vegetable garden. The pavement is swept clean, cats are taking their "before supper" stroll, the windows of the surrounding houses are filled with clay pots in which geraniums and *Asparagus plumosus* are dying from lack of water. The district is second-class but it is altogether not so bad, I think. I wave back to the little old lady who smiles at me as she sits behind a wrought-iron fence in a small garden and knits socks, her face frail and transparent like a china doll's. The hotel porter tells me that Herr Zuckerman lives on the third floor but that the elevator is out of order. So I begin climbing the stairs. The steps are rather steep and I pause for a while on the first landing, my heart pounding. I think how much I would rather be elsewhere than here on these insignificant stairs that smell of the surrounding rooms. They smell of old wood and of old dust and legions of people who have occupied them before and still do. The rooms smell of digested and undigested food and the variously textured skin of their occupants. For some reason, scenes from my life are coming to the front of my mind in crystal-clear images as if I were dying.

The scent of acacia trees and of the garden surrounding my old home by the Danube back in Esztergom come to my nostrils as vividly as if I were there now in person. I see the sky of my childhood put together miraculously with lights and textures of golds and blues. Then I am back to reality again, diligently climbing up to the third floor, wishing all the time that I was going down instead of up. Now the colorless face of the hotel porter comes to my mind illogically. I take a deep breath and continue my way up brave like a soldier. I force myself to knock on the door.

"C'mon in. It's open." A voice invites me inside with an aggressive yet tired tone. As I enter the room I am taken aback. I expected a normal hotel room with basic furniture in it, but all I can see are patches of light and shadows as if I were somewhere at the bottom of the sea, alone. Then a man comes forward from the window where the light from outside made him invisible. Somehow, I sense danger. The whole scene resembles a snapshot I had once seen of a place somewhere in New Guinea with cannibals hiding in the tall grass.

My eyes are blurred from anxiety, yet he looks human as he approaches, a medium-sized man bruised by middle age, thin and undernourished. He is dressed in a colorless something, which blends perfectly into the room… grays and dark grays and faded brown tones dominating.

Suddenly, I see everything in sharp focus as if I were Pinkerton from Scotland Yard inspecting the scene of a mysterious murder. He smiles at me as if to win me over. I introduce myself and he nods politely. I mention Maca's name, which he acknowledges matter-of-factly. He then walks to a desk from which he takes out papers and manilla envelopes. He shows me the typewriter in the middle of the room. He asks me to copy some contracts. I sit down and I try very hard but I don't understand a word of what I am typing, being unfamiliar with business terms. He watches over my shoulder very closely. I am disturbed by his closeness and make more mistakes. The sentences flow into each other before my eyes.

What could be wrong with this man, I ask myself, as he stands closely behind me, so close that I feel his breath on the nape of my neck. I don't know if he wants to grab me or hit me. I try to chase away the bad thoughts and I struggle with the text while I feel him pacing behind me. I relax a bit when he excuses himself to go to the toilet, but when he returns and locks the door I become alarmed again. While he was out of the room I thought about the money I could make, which would allow me to take a trip to Switzerland to visit Tibor in the sanitorium. I have the lucky ability of switching my thoughts quickly, putting the bad ones away and allowing the good ones in. I began to apologize for my lousy typing and try to forget about the locked door. I thought if I could keep on talking I would think of a way to leave quickly.

"Nonsense," he replies to my apologies. "You are doing quite well. What we both need is to relax a bit."

He is touching me now with his fingers. I jump up in surprise.

"I want to make love to you," he says.

I bump into my chair, which falls down with a loud noise.

"I will pay you for everything," he says and I'm not sure what he means. He begins to undress, quickly peeling off his shirt and pants and underwear, impatiently and with jerky movements as though he were peeling off the skin of an apple with a razor. My eyes are glued to his abdomen where he has a surgical scar about five inches long.

"Please don't do anything to me!" I beg him, my voice weak.

He drags me to his bed.

I wanted to scream but no one would ever hear me or pay attention. The dark lobbies outside are deserted.

I thought of the accomplice smile of the porter downstairs.

Maybe he knew about the whole thing! I might not be the only one who came to type for Mr. Zuckerman. There may be a long line of girls coming up the stairs to Room 23— a long line of victims, I think. But how does Maca fit into all this?

I don't have time to figure it out.

I lie on his bed like a rag doll in a daze, unable to move.

"I'm still a virgin, you know," I tell him with extreme difficulty. Without answering, he goes to the night table and pours himself a glass of water from a pitcher… his hands trembling. That is the only sign that he must be also human. Perhaps he is as uncomfortable as I am.

He comes back and he throws himself on top of me.

I feel his clammy fingers and I smell his stale breath.

I wish I could cry out hysterically, but I grit my teeth together in silence.

The pain in my body is as sharp as if someone was cutting me with the edge of a razor.

He breathes heavily as he… finishes his task.

It is all over now. All over.

He took everything he wanted from me, and more.

I feel barren like the earth in ashes after an engulfing forest fire that has destroyed the trees.

He stole from me everything I had been saving to give to the man I loved.

He robbed me from my dreams, irretrievably.

I am a woman now with full knowledge, expelled from Paradise.

He sits on the edge of the bed now, defiant and rebellions like Adam might have been after committing the original sin.

He lets his arms go limp as he stares into the air in a daze as though he was drunk or as if he had just returned from a tiring yet thrilling journey from a lush and tropical island.

I could tell he was slightly grateful that I hadn't put up any resistance. He hadn't the slightest idea that when he took me into his possession, I wasn't with him but with Tibor. I feel a great despair that Tibor wasn't the one to make me his woman.

In my mind I have a vision that I am standing by a gravesite where something precious is buried, questioning the harsh autumn wind that blows the mawkish fumes of wax candles toward my face.

Why did it happen to me? Was I cursed? I get dressed slowly, tired as if I had just returned from climbing Mount Everest.

He reaches for his wallet on the night table and takes out three one hundred Schilling bills so as to pay me.

"Buy something nice for yourself, a bottle of perfume or a Pucci scarf or whatever," he says.

A sense of relief comes over me, which can be equated to happiness, as I step outside the door and gain my freedom from the lion's cage.

I hurry down the stairs and outside to the street to find that nothing has changed. People are hurrying home for supper, strolling under the gray shadows of the trees, their faces illuminated by the pale lights. Crowds of men gather in front of a nightclub, they stare at the photos of Oriental and Swedish and American beauties, whose erotic smiles are framed behind the glass and at the photos of nude girls who will be part of the *tableau vivant* show tonight.

The city goes on its way as if nothing had happened. It is only I who am filled with bitter thoughts. No one pays any attention to me. I get occasional neutral glances from someone passing by, from clerks and artists, maids and call girls, pimps and gigolos who fill the streets. No one from that ocean of people has the slightest idea that I am not the same as I was before, that something inside had snapped. The night policeman who stands on guard at the gate of the barracks greets me with a friendly smile.

"*Gute nacht, schönes fräulein!*"‡‡ he says and his blue eyes show admiration as always when he sees me, as he politely opens the gates. He doesn't even ask for my identification card because I am his innocent flirt. He is full of goodwill and he smiles as he gives me some more compliments, expecting some nice words from me in return as usual.

‡‡ Goodnight, beautiful young lady

Tonight I pass him in a hurry. I don't want him to notice that I am not the same person I was before, not the gay and happy and friendly creature I was only yesterday.

Once in my cubicle, I grab a towel and some soap and I go to the shower room to take a long cleansing hot shower.

Back in my room, I lie on my cot thinking things over in retrospect. I place the three hundred Schillings on top of the table beside my cot. They look like flat green frogs with slippery, ice-cold bodies. I have never liked frogs. They gave me the creeps in the school laboratory when we had to dissect them…

I don't want to look at the money and I would rather not think of what happened earlier today. Yet I remember everything crystal clear that took place back in the hotel room.

Thoughts are coming to my mind indiscriminately and in a big variety, as if they were the colored particles of a kaleidoscope.

The pain I feel in my body also reminds me of what happened, as well as the blood that is still dripping from me like tiny red pearls.

The eyes of Tibor are coming to my aid now, his golden-brown eyes spotted with green like a tortoiseshell, loving eyes in the depth of which I can always find forgiveness and understanding.

Now the spring meadows of my childhood come back to my mind. I walk on the meandering streets of the small sleepy city amid the clangor of the big bells. The sounds of the bells lie on the pavement heavy like stones. The huge marble pillars in front of the Cathedral high up on the hill are like the huge hands of God, held erect and pointing toward the sky, where cumulus clouds swim with dreamy slowness.

I pace the rooms of our long, grayish-white house by the Danube where I was so happy with Father, and where as long as Mother was there, there was always a good time and good eating; crickets chirped in the garden under the shady trees, a wild elder tree perfumed the air, and the fish-smelling breath of the Danube balanced the sweet scent of the garden.

Sister Agnes' soft round face appears on the screen of my past, the one who taught us religion and Latin. She told us that nothing really bad can happen to us in the course of our lives if we only trust in God.

She told us that if something bad did happen, God would give us the strength to survive everything, no matter how badly we are hurt by sickness or bad luck or anything.

I feel as though I now belong to the category of losers. Yet I can't question God as to why he let me go through all that sadness because life has also brought me much joy and happiness and good things. Everything balances itself, Mother used to say. No one can have everything. Life has its ups and downs, "that is life!"

The final conclusion is that I possess something valuable, no matter how naked and exploited I feel at present.

I have an immeasurable amount of love I received in the past from Father and Mother and Grandmother, embedded deep down in my bone marrow. I feel warm and alive from its flame and I glow by its light like a lightning bug, becoming strong and indestructible at the same time. Therefore, nothing and no one can destroy me, not even the man who robbed me of so much.

It will be easy to erase him from my mind— it will be easy.

I will never think about him and his burned-out-volcano eyes.

I will try very hard— I will try.

That's enough of that man!

I touch the gold amulet on my neck, which belonged to Grandmother, and I lightly stroke the engraved words on it. I stroke the words with my soul as well as with my fingertips… repeating with my lips, *"OMNIA VINCIT AMOR."*[§§]

Now I must make plans for the future.

I have much to do. I must do what I have wanted to do for a long time but never did, and now is the time to do it!

I must write down the story of the Hungarian freedom fighters who gave their life for *freedom*.

I must tell their stories to the free world before the story gets lost… I am very tired now but I feel uplifted as if I had drunk cups and cups of strong espresso coffee, or as if I had a cup of strong mulled wine, while in reality I haven't even had supper.

I am not sure whether it's a trick of my tired nerves or reality when I hear footsteps approaching.

Then I see two sunburned hands lifting up the faded curtain that serves as a door on the opening of my niche. I recognize him in the faded light. "Oh my love!" I cry. "You came when I needed you the most and not a moment too soon."

---

§§   LOVE CONQUERS ALL

EPILOGUE

I BOARDED the old, four engine USA military plane from West Germany, Munich, on a snowy winter morning, along with about 200 other refugees from the Albrecht refugee camp. The inevitable reporters were there, flashing their cameras, trying to catch the expressions on our faces as we walked in a daze through the gates. Taking photographs of the refugees in all kinds of situations was *"de rigueur"* during those days of exodus when 200,000 of us lived in various camps all over in Austria. We monopolized the headlines.

It took about 16 hours to get to New York on the rickety plane. We landed once in Shannon, Ireland, and once in New Foundland.

I was scared and fatigued from my first flight over the Atlantic, yet I was filled with unspeakable excitement, and also anticipation.

I still remember every minute as if it were yesterday, the moment when we landed at the International Airport, which smelled of fuel and snowclouds. My heart was beating fast, it was one of the most cherished moments in my life.

Some of the refugees had tears in their eyes, a young Jewish woman knelt down and kissed the shining, cold floor of the waiting room. There was glory and happiness on the faces of the members of "slave society" arriving in the land of individual freedom.

    I vividly recall the wonder I felt seeing the big metropolis, the lights of New York, the cave-like streets and tall, box-like buildings made out of steel and glass, standing tall and erect like the elongated fingers of some pagan God. New York seemed different from the big citys I'd seen in Europe, it seemed more dynamic, full of life. Everyone was in a big hurry except the pidgeons, who were everywhere, even on the windowsills, watching with melancholy eyes the newspapers that flew in the wind. I was enchanted by the varied color of the people, ranging from white to copper to black, and I loved the huge billboard on Broadway where a rosy-cheeked man blew smoke from his paper lips beneath the letters "Camel cigarettes."

    I missed Tibor and felt sad that he hadn't been able to come with me, that we couldn't enjoy the sensation and sweetness of our very first moments in America. He had had to go back to the sanatorium from where he had sneaked out for a few days just to be with me.

    Of course life wasn't easy without him, especially at the beginning. Sometimes I felt I was a fool to have succumbed to his will urging me to go alone, sometimes I almost cursed him because I missed him so badly.

    I got a job soon after I arrived in Cincinnati. I was a waitress in a dark-green, damp garden restaurant. The proprietor, a big, husky, red-faced German made me put away dozens of stone-heavy wooden chairs after every party, taking advantage of the fact that I was a newcomer and didn't speak English. My muscles and bones ached, yet I received generous tips from kind Americans when I served their dinner. With the money I bought books from which I could I earn English. I could also afford to buy food, and rent a room up in the attic of a two-story family house where the landlady was kind enough to lend me her kitchen to cook my breakfast.

In the beginning I ate only one meal a day, the phenomenal American breakfast that was more nourishing and satisfying then the cup of tea and slice of bread I used to have in Europe. The strong cup of coffee, bacon and eggs, orange juice and buttered rolls kept me going all day long. For supper I usually had some boiled potatoes, because money was tight those days. Money was scarce and my fears mounted, not because of money but because letters from Vienna were arriving less and less.

Meanwhile I wrote sheets of letters to Tibor, describing my new life in the States, trying to give a true picture of my new country. I wrote him how everything here was different, including the houses which were built of wood and looked fragile as if they could be easily blown away with the wind…

"The trees are taller here," I wrote, "and the vegetation is greener and more dense. The countryside is always sparkling green. The people are kind and generous. It's a wonderful world. I simply adore it! I am very much upset without you," I wrote, "I am crying, that's how I spend my nights."

I felt dying when his letters ceased to come. It happened during the time of silence when I met a dark haired young man at an ethnic dance. Years later he asked me to marry him.

And so I did.

Now I almost have everything I ever wanted. The most important thing is that I have a free life in a free country. The freedom in America is taller than the tallest trees. It reaches the sky and beyond. It is immeasurable, like space. Sometimes I even feel that I can't comprehend it, maybe because I was brought up in the shadow of the Soviet army and the Hungarian secret police.

I have a golden haired daughter, named Rita. She is a true native of practical America— thank God. I know that she loves me, yet she has a hint of criticism in her sea-blue eyes if I spend too much time in my garden daydreaming. My garden is like a jungle, overgrown with wild azaleas and lilies, and all kind of bushes. My heart is overgrown with memories, with appreciation of all the years of my life made up of layers of good and bad, and I just wouldn't change every blessed moment of it.

* * *

The end.

AFTERWORD

IRENE KORPONAY HAS HAD a good life in America. Her daughter married an American engineer and gave her three beautiful grandchildren. Her youngest grandson edited and self-published this book. Without him, this would not have been possible. She is also now a great grandmother of two little boys.

Printed in Dunstable, United Kingdom